BUILDING BETTER THEATERS

Michael Mell

ENTERTAINMENT TECHNOLOGY PRESS

Consultancy Series

BUILDING BETTER THEATERS

Michael Mell

Entertainment Technology Press

Building Better Theaters

© Michael Mell

First edition published May 2006
Revised January 2008
by Entertainment Technology Press Ltd
The Studio, High Green, Great Shelford, Cambridge CB22 5EG
Internet: www.etnow.com

ISBN 978 1 904031 40 6

A title within the
Entertainment Technology Press Consultancy Series
Series editor: John Offord

CODE / BBT02-0308

CONTENTS

ACKNOWLEDGEMENTS

We are all formed and molded by the persons we meet and I would like to give some of them credit here.

Albert and Marion Mell, Susan Mell, Bruce Robertson, Kathy Kennedy, Joan Olsson, Dr. Joel Rubin, Jackie Staines, John Offord, Ted Abromov, Cliff Simon, Michael Friedman, Barbara Bauer, Richard and Jackie Dunham, John Darren, Dr. Gary Gaiser, Jan Hise, Joe Baer, Steve Rader, Lou Shapiro, Peter Erskine, Robert Branningan, Robert Lorelli, Sonny and Kelly Sonnenfeld, Chris Blair, Luiz Felizardo, Jose Neopmuceno, Acuna Sole, Maria Alba Fisch and lastly, my wife Kate and my sons Sam and Tyler.

PREFACE

I suppose there are some people who know what they want to do with their lives from an early age. Some early childhood career choices, such as fireman, doctor and teacher, are actually pursued into adulthood. For most of us the path to our adult career is a journey to an unknown destination. Only by looking back can we trace our path and, as the poet says, the road not taken.

My path started in the autumn of 1968 when, at age thirteen, I joined the theater group at the local "Y". I no longer remember the reason for my initial attraction. Outside of attendance at a few orchestra concerts and school plays I had never seen a professional theater production. Whatever the reason, it was a brave new world and I had a great time. Active in the theater group for four years, working with my friends to present plays was a very enjoyable and stimulating part of my life, but it was only one activity among many. At the same time I also attended school, went to summer camp, went to the movies, watched lots of television and experienced the trials and tribulations unique to being a teenager.

Senior year in high school brought SATs and GREs, a driver's license, applications to colleges and the quandary of what to do with my life, what kind of job would I like; would I be able to get it and how much would it pay? One of the older members of the theater group was already in college and, of course, all of us went to see the first production he was involved in. Afterward, he walked me through the backstage, the scene shop, costume shop, prop shop and studio theater. I'm sure I was drooling. The stage at the "Y" was at one end of a large flat-floor multipurpose room. The stage had no wings, no fly space, no rigging system, no lighting system and no sound system. The sparking of our rented Edkotron dimmer pack was often more exciting then the lighting onstage.

I had always thought that working in the theater, while a wonderful part of my life, had to be put aside for college and the pursuit of "real" work. As my friend told me about the different classes he was taking as a theater major, I was overcome with euphoria. Not only could I continue to "do shows", but would now get college credit for it. Not only could I study theater in college, but could get paid to work in the theater afterwards. I was in heaven.

My life did not enfold exactly as I envisioned 35 years ago. My fireplace mantle is not lined with Tony Awards for lighting design. I do not live in Manhattan but sixty miles north in the lower Hudson Valley. As anyone given a chance to re-live their lives would, I would likely make some choices differently but not too many.

The lessons I learned at the "Y" are still with me and remain a touchstone in my consulting practice. It is not the space, per se, or the theatrical technology that makes "theater." They are only the tools used by artists to create.

Michael Mell
March, 2006

INTRODUCTION

Since the creation of spoken language, human beings have had the need and desire to communicate, to tell a story. One only has to look at people, from all walks of life, performing all of life's tasks with a cell phone glued to their ear. Earlier in our history story telling was a much simpler affair. We can imagine our ancestors, gathered around a fire, listening to tales of the day's hunt. Over time, story-telling became more than an account of daily activities; it became a forum to explore the world. Soon special places were dedicated to telling stories and drama was born.

From Greek amphitheaters and Roman coliseums, to the use of perspective during the Italian Renaissance, to Shakespeare's Globe Theatre, to the Drottningholm Theater, Wagner's Bayreuth, Appia and Craig, Walter Gropius and the Bauhaus School, Broadway, Josef Svoboda, Peter Brook, The Living Theater of the 1960s … all have sought to re-define drama and the places where it is performed.

Over time, theaters (which I shall use to stand for the many different types of performing arts facilities) have been built by many agencies and for many reasons (of which the presentation of a theatrical event has often been the least!). The size, cost and sheer magnitude of the undertaking have limited the building of theaters to individuals and groups with a great deal of money and political power. In the historic past this group was small and included only monarchs and municipalities (i.e. various European city-states). Today, the group includes: federal, state and municipal governments, colleges and universities, corporations and philanthropists, well established performing arts groups … well, you get the picture. These groups build theaters with a capital T. The intent is to create large scale venues seating large numbers of people.

The past 60 years or so have seen theaters created in many different kinds of spaces, by individuals and small groups with limited budgets. They can be found in church basements, shopping malls, office buildings, parking garages, barns, tents and outdoor spaces. These theaters, with a lower case t, are less interested in where their performances take place or how large the audience might be. This is not to say one is better or more desirable than the other. Both small and large theaters have their virtues and drawbacks and I will not pass any judgment. I will say that there can be as many kinds of theater buildings as there are people who wish to use them and this is a good thing.

The proliferation of smaller, ad hoc theaters has, in a sense, returned us to the camp fire in that drama becomes an activity for everyone to participate in.

Regardless of the scale of the theater, building codes, the Americans with Disabilities Act (ADA) and technology have, without malice, conspired to make the creation of a place of assembly (that's code-speak for a theater) a process that requires the use of many specialized consultants. The Design Team includes: architects, engineers, code consultants, ADA consultants, acousticians and, of course, theater consultants. All have unique experience and expertise that is required for the design and construction of a theater. They/we are all tools to be used by you ... the owner. You are the reason we are all here. It's your theater and, within the constraints of budget and local politics, you should get everything you want. There is only one drawback: the owner has to make all the decisions. Theaters are very complex buildings and the decision to build one is only the first of thousands of choices that you will have to make.

In my experience very few owners have the opportunity to be involved in the design or renovation of one theater, let alone two. As owner you are ultimately responsible for the successful completion of your theater. How do you find out what to do? The answer is simple ... education. You have been trained in

Figure 1: Amphitheatre.

your field of choice, so doesn't it stand to reason you should train yourself in the process of designing a theater? You don't need a BA in Architecture, but you should know what a massing model is. As I mentioned earlier, we are your tools and we can't work by ourselves; a hammer doesn't pound a nail until the carpenter picks it up.

An old television commercial ended with a somber-voiced man intoning: "An educated consumer is our best customer". Quite frankly, the more you know the easier it is for the Design Team to do its job and the more motivated we can be. This is the reason I decided to write this book. As a theater consultant, I want to make your life easier as you embark upon the creation of your theater.

1 PUTTING ON A ~~SHOW~~ BUILDING

It's the same ... only different.

When I was first out of graduate school, in the late 1970s, I worked for Theater Design & Technology, a sound system design and rental firm. At the time one of the owners, Lou Shapiro, was designing many Broadway shows. He returned to the office, one afternoon, looking a little hang-dog and said: "Everybody knows two things, their business... and sound". We all looked knowingly at each other because what Lou had said was consistent with what we experienced every day. Today I would modify the phrase and substitute theater consulting for sound.

It is not uncommon to hear this sentiment voiced "...we work in the theater every day – we know what we want ... why do we need to hire a consultant?" Doesn't the technical director know about stage layout? Don't the scenic, lighting, costume and sound designers know their needs? Doesn't the House Manager know what is needed in the lobby? Well, yes they do. They all know about working in a theater. They all know how to "put on a show". What they may not know is how to "put on a building". Although there are similarities between the two, there are also significant differences.

A show is just one particular show. Within the confines of a given venue, all efforts are directed toward fulfilling the needs of the show and that show only. The run of a show may be open-ended but is, ultimately, finite. A performing arts building has to satisfy many masters. It may have to accommodate drama, musical theater, dance, ballet, opera and symphony orchestras as well as unknown user groups, touring shows, other attractions. The facility must be flexible so that it may grow, over time, to satisfy what the future may bring. The "run" of a performing arts building can range from 30-100 years.

The design team for a show includes: a director, technical director, lighting, costume, scenic and sound designers. Most likely they have all worked together and, even if not, they all have the same grounding in how to mount a production and have been involved in many shows. The design team for a performing arts facility includes: architect, owner, structural engineer, mechanical engineer, electrical engineer, civil engineer, theater consultant, acoustician, lighting consultant and code consultant – to name but a few. The larger the facility is; the more the players who will be involved. Most likely they have not all worked together before and, even if they have, performing arts facilities are all unique and complex (even though they may share certain infrastructure requirements).

The approach to designing a show also differs from designing a building. A theatrical production generally includes: design meetings, rehearsals, load-in, technical rehearsals, dress rehearsals and opening night. A production schedule, from beginning to end may last two to six months. The sequence of events for designing a building is more specific and has been codified by organizations such as the American Institute of Architects (AIA) and local, state and federal agencies. The design sequence for a performing arts building may include: programming, site selection, schematic design, design development, construction documentation, bidding, shop drawing review, construction and final inspection. Design and construction may take anywhere from two to six years.

The Players

The design team for a performing arts facility has its own unique cast of characters that differ from those involved in putting on a show. They typically include: architect, owner, structural engineer, mechanical engineer, electrical engineer, civil engineer, theater consultant and acoustician. A large or multi-venue facility might also include: code consultant, cost consultant, lighting consultant, interior designer, parking consultant, signage consultant, ADA consultant and art consultant. Each of these represent an individual group that may comprise from one to twenty people (and you thought your production meetings were unwieldy!). Who are these people and what, exactly, do they do? Although there are exceptions, a brief, partial description is listed below.

> **Architect** – overall design of the facility, hiring and coordination of the other design team members and legal responsibility to meet all applicable codes and regulations. The architect will often hire the theater consultant and acoustician (more about this later).

> **Owner** (that's you!) – the person or agency responsible for initiating the creation of a theater in the first place. Also the entity that holds the purse strings.

> **Structural engineer** – design of structure (building steel, rigging steel, catwalks, galleries, concrete foundations, footings, etc.) They make sure the building won't fall down.

Mechanical engineer – design of heating and ventilation (HVAC) systems. Also responsible for plumbing and sprinkler systems.

Electrical engineer – design of electrical systems and equipment (power to building, power infrastructure, emergency power, security systems, general lighting, incorporation of stage lighting and sound systems prepared by theater consultant, fire alarm system, telephone and data ... anything that uses electricity.

Civil engineer – evaluation of site and necessary preparations for the site to accept the building.

Theater consultant (They are your friends!) – works with the design team on planning of facility and design of theater equipment and systems. Responsibilities include: stage and backstage layout, seating and sightlines, design and specification of stage lighting, audience seating, stage rigging and motorized stage machinery. Also reviews shop drawings, monitors construction, inspects and tests theatrical equipment and provides quality assurance. Makes sure that, at the end of the day, the completed project will be functional for all the people who will work there.

Acoustician (S/he is your friend too!) – works with the design team to shape the audience chamber and its interior finishes to provide the required acoustic response (for the program). Also provides noise criteria for the mechanical systems and ensures that they are followed.

Code consultant – advises design team about interpreting and satisfying local, state and federal codes and ADA.

Cost consultant – monitors project cost throughout design and assists the design team should the project go over-budget.

ADA consultant – works with the design team to satisfy the requirements of the Americans with Disabilities Act are met, as well as, requirements of local Persons With Disabilities (PWD) advocacy groups.

The chain of command starts with you. It is your responsibility to participate throughout the entire process. You are the person with the most intimate knowledge of how the facility will operate and will be living with the decisions you make for many years. The theater consultant's experience in the architectural design process will ensure that seemingly small decisions during schematic design don't snowball into large problems during construction documents or during construction (when they are difficult and much more costly to remedy). The design team wants to design a facility that fits your unique needs – now and in the future – and they will welcome your input.

2 DOING YOUR HOMEWORK

The design team is comprised of many imaginative and creative people, all dedicated to the creation of your theater. We can do many things; but we can't read minds. You must do your homework so that you can act as an informed client. If you don't know what your homework is, we can help to identify and refine questions and recommend directions to proceed in.

The design team will not/cannot/should not make final decisions for you nor can they be expected to take full responsibility for the outcome of the design. You must remain an active member of the team, bringing your knowledge of the theater's needs to the table for discussion and incorporation into the design. We need the information that only you can provide. The better prepared you are, the better prepared we can be and the easier it will be for the design team to put our expertise to work for you.

Like any group endeavor the design process is also a political process, but not everyone's agenda may have the creation of a functional performance facility at the top of the list. There are a number of things you can/should do to support yourself and your opinions during the design process.

Making It Happen

People are afraid of new things and of change in general. It is easier (and safer) to find reasons not to do something. It takes courage to do something new, especially in the face of opposition. Margaret Mead, the noted anthropologist, once said: "It always takes a dedicated group of people to make anything worthwhile happen". You must assemble an advocacy group to make your project happen. Depending upon your situation, that group may include some of the following people: elected officials, business leaders, philanthropists, college dean, provost or president, groups that will benefit (theater, ballet, modern dance, symphony, opera, etc.), prominent community figures, and persons who have contributed to other arts organizations and facilities. A strong advocacy group will have the focused commitment and tenacity required to build a performing arts facility.

One of the common tools used to demonstrate the desirability and viability of a theater is to commission a Feasibility Study. This type of study is usually performed by a team that includes an architect, theater consultant, management consultant and cost consultant. A successful study will provide the information needed to make intelligent decisions about the construction, renovation, restoration or adaptive re-use of a theater. The first portion generally includes: analysis of the market area, consideration of possible uses and users of potential facilities, an inventory of other regional facilities, and assessment of the possible impacts and benefits. Following that information is: criteria for site selection, building massing, preliminary space planning, organizational adjacencies, building footprint, utilities, parking and a construction budget. A comprehensive study will also include: governance, staffing, facility operation, community access, pro-forma operating budgets, economic impact, and ongoing funding. Feasibility studies can last a few weeks, a few months or over a year, depending upon its scope.

Decide What You Want Your Facility to Do

A common pitfall among owners and user groups is using a new theater to solve problems in their current venues. The new theater represents a clean slate that is waiting to be written upon by you. It's a time to think outside the box and inside the box. Which things do you believe work and which don't? What activities and events are anticipated in the first years after opening day? After ten years? Twenty years? The theater you create will be around for many years, but you will not. Don't preclude anything just because it is not your preferred method or approach.

There is a great deal of information available and many new and interesting technologies. It is easy to miss the forest for the trees. For a renovation or new

ITEM	SPACE	NOTES	NSF
5.00	**TECHINCAL SUPPORT SPACES**	SLLs and wheelchair access are not included	
5.01	Lighting and sound control room	Direct access to audience chamber, and sound equipment room	300
5.02	Announce/Observation/Stage Manager's room	Rear of main floor at center line	80
5.03	Projection room	Toilet and dedicated technical access	350
5.04	Followspot room	Toilet, dedicated technical access and access for large equipment	300
5.05	Staff toilet	Adjacent to control rooms	50
5.06	Amplifier rack room	At or near attic level in close proximity to loudspeaker clusters	100
5.07	Dimmer room	Between audience chamber and stage house at upper level	250
5.08	Technical circulation	Includes circulation between: orchestra pit, stage, all control rooms and lighting positions	IG
	SUB-TOTAL		**1,430**

Figure 2: Detail of Space Plan.

facility to replace an existing one, look at your current system and how it is used. What works and what doesn't? What new demands can you see in the immediate and far future? Are there any safety concerns?

Budget

It is the lucky owner who gets everything they want – and I have never met any lucky ones. Whether the budget is $3 million or $200 million, there never seems to be enough money. Develop a budget based on the goals you wish to achieve. Again, talk with your theater consultant. Leave some wiggle room in your budget – remember it is almost impossible to get more money, but you will certainly be asked to spend less.

One important budget item that is often omitted is a contingency. Despite the "best laid plans of architects and consultants", it is inevitable that something will be overlooked. A contingency is an allowance of 5-10% of the projected construction budget to be used for unforeseen costs. A new site or a change in program or the unforeseen consequence of early design choices or simply a better idea may cause an increase in the projected cost of the theater. A design contingency is intended to address these costs. During construction unanticipated field conditions (i.e. when they start to dig that big hole in the ground) may cause an increase in costs. Contractor change orders (discussed in chapter 7) for ambiguous or omitted items in the bid drawings and specifications may also increase costs. A construction contingency is intended to address these costs.

Even if your design and construction budgets include suitable contingencies you should not become complacent. When the monetary push comes to shove, as it certainly will, the first thing to go will be the contingency funds. It only makes sense, right? The reduction or elimination of the contingency will have no impact upon the building. No one will have to sacrifice their cherished concerns (marble floors in the lobby and the lighting control console that also bakes bread and makes coffee). In the euphoria of the design, when all things seem possible, it may appear that nothing can go wrong and surely things will continue to proceed smoothly. DON'T BET ON IT! Death, taxes and Murphy's Law (*The worst possible thing will happen at the worst possible moment*) are the three certainties in this life. Don't let anyone try to convince you that your project will be the exception to the rule. On a more serious note, the political and financial realities of building a theater may lead you to make this choice. If you decide to eliminate the contingencies, make as informed a decision as you can and always remember that it is a calculated risk.

TYPICAL PROJECT BUDGET ITEMS

ITEM	ESTIMATE	ITEM	ESTIMATE
Estimate Construction Contract	$	Clean-Up	
Architecture & Engineering Fees		Security	
NIC Construction Costs		Project Supervision	
Movable Equipment & Operating Supplies		Total $	
Food & Beverage Equipment			
Lobby & Pre-Function Furnishings		MOVABLE EQUIPMENT	
Startup costs			
Total $		Itemized Movable Equipment	
		Initial Operating Supplies	
CONSTRUCTION CONTRACT		Public Address System	
		Telephone System	
Contract Amount		Equipment Specification Fees	
Change Order Reserve		Purchasing Fees	
Contingencies		Freight	
Total $		Contingencies	
		Total $	
ARCHITECTURE & ENGINEERING FEES			
		FOOD & BEVERAGE EQUIPMENT	
Architectural Contract			
Architect Reimburseables		Kitchen Equipment	
Program Consultant		Beverage Equipment	
Mechanical/Electrical/HVAC		Concessions Equipment	
Structural Engineer		Total $	
Civil Engineer			
Lighting Consultant		LOBBY & PRE-FUNCTION	
Graphics Consultant			
Interior Design Consultant		Furniture	
Theater Consultant		Interior Landscaping	
Acoustics Consultant		Draperies	
Audio-Visual Consultant		Total $	
Landscaping Consultant			
Food & Beverage Consultant		STARTUP COSTS	
Elevator Consultant			
Code Consultant		Salaries & Benefits	
Energy Consultant		Contract Services	
Parking/Traffic Consultant		Dues & Subscriptions	
Consultant Reimbursables		Recruitment Expenses	
Testing & Special Inspections		Employee Relocation	
Photos & Blueprints		Office Rental	
Rendering/Models		Equipment Rental	
Total $		Interim Signage	
		Office Supplies & Printing	
NIC CONSTRUCTION COSTS		Maintenance Supplies	
		Advertising & Promotion	
Permits & Fees		Postage & Freight	
Bonds & Insurance		Travel Expenses	
Exterior Landscaping, Irrigation, Lighting		Utilities	
Exterior Graphics		Telephone (Local & Long-Distance)	
Interior Graphics		Security	
Millwork, Counters, Cabinets, Shelving		Pre-Opening Expenses	
		Total Cost $	

Figure 3: Typical project budget.

Capital Costs vs. Operational Costs

In the preceding section we discussed all the elements (i.e. capital costs) that go into the construction of the building, commonly known as 'bricks and mortar". Operational costs are those expenses that will be incurred in the day-to-day operation of the theater. Operational funding comes from three primary sources.

- Earned Income includes: ticket sales, festival profits, souvenir sales, rentals to outside groups, liquor and food concessions and similar items.
- Contributed Income includes: individual and corporate donations and endowments.
- Public Support includes: funding from any city, state or federal agency.

Fig. 3, Typical Project Budget identifies some initial operational costs as 'start up costs'. As the name implies, these expenses are necessary to get things going and will bridge the construction and the opening of the theater. These may appear to be separate and discreet budgets, but as in the Big Bang, when all aspects of the universe were one aspect: in the Big Bang of the design of the theater they are intertwined. As the universe expanded and different aspects came into being; the untwining of capital and operational costs will have a very concrete and long lasting impact upon the theater.

A common example is whether to install a motorized orchestra pit lift or use infill platforms. The cost of the lift, itself, can run $250,000 and $500,000 while platforms may only cost $75,000 to $150,000. If you are looking at ways of reducing your construction (i.e. capital) budget, this is definitely an option worth considering. Remember, however, that this capital saving will be transferred to the operational budget in the form of increased labor costs and these costs will forever be a part of the theater's budget. One choice is not inherently better or worse than the other and, as we have discussed, each theater will have its own unique set of conditions. The 'right' decision needs to be taken in the context of the project as a whole.

Expectations

Understand that the design of a theater is a collaborative process and there will be, of necessity, much give and take. You will not get everything you want, when you want it, the way you want it. Don't feel bad – no one involved will get everything. You will find, if you have your priorities in order that you will get what you need (apologies to the Rolling Stones). An apparent set-back can lead you in unexpected directions. Don't hold a grudge and keep an open mind. Remember that everyone involved is working toward the same goal.

Educate Your Design Team

Just as you documented and justified the need for a theater, to the powers-that-be, you must be able to communicate your needs to the design team. Be prepared to respond when someone says, "… but how often do you need to do that?" Be prepared to explain why a front-of-house lighting catwalk is better than a motorized batten that must be repeatedly raised and lowered to focus the stage lighting. Be prepared to explain why the loading dock cannot be ten feet above stage level in a road house.

Your theater consultant will likely lead the charge when these issues arise, but we are only human. Sometimes we can get into a rut about doing certain things a certain way. Again, we are tools that you must use.

Stay Involved

Designing a performance facility is a long and drawn-out process. Unforeseen obstacles will occur. Budgets will be reduced and may or may not be restored. The price of steel may skyrocket (as it did in the early 2000s) and knock the project budget for a loop. You may grow to love the people you are working with. You may grow to hate the people you are working with. You may get bored. You may want to throw up your hands in disgust. Whatever you do, stay involved. Remember, when the project is complete all the unpleasant memories will fade away and the friends you have made and the excitement of creation will remain.

3 ASSEMBLING YOUR TEAM

Selecting the Architect

Selection of the architect and design team is, perhaps, the most critical decision you will make. The planning of a theater is a high profile project, especially in small communities. If project funding comes from a Bond Issue, then the community's investment is even greater. Today there are many architectural firms with large experience in the design of performing arts facilities. The advantages of this hands-on experience are great; the primary being not having to re-invent the wheel. Politics may require that this "design" architect be affiliated with a local firm that will perform part of the work (usually construction drawings, specifications and construction administration). In addition, the local architect provides valuable knowledge of site conditions, contractors, availability of labor skills and materials.

When is the best time to hire an architect? There is no rule-of-thumb. Some projects select the architect before fundraising has begun. Others wait until the project funding is in place and all preliminary studies and programming is complete. Municipal agencies and colleges and universities may have a very specific, rigid procedure. The financial, organizational and political considerations of your project will determine the best time. Experience and expertise aside, there should be an emotional connection – that ineffable, gut feeling that tells you that this is the right architect for your project.

Some things you want/need to know in selecting an architect or theater consultant

General Information
- ✓ Firm or firms involved
- ✓ Team composition
- ✓ Attitude and reputation
- ✓ Design vision for your project

Personnel
- ✓ Principal-in-charge
- ✓ Project architect and design
- ✓ Examples of completed work
- ✓ Consultants

Experience
- ✓ General project experience
- ✓ Experience in projects similar to yours
- ✓ Experience of individual design team members

Performance
- ✓ Proposed method of working on your project
- ✓ Current work load and ability to devote sufficient time and staff to project architects
- ✓ Previous team experience
- ✓ Cost control/cost management practices
- ✓ Recent bidding experience
- ✓ References

Figure 4: Architect selection check-list.

Selecting the Theater Consultant

Here I must confess my bias as a working theater consultant that, when is comes to designing a theater, we are the best thing since sliced bread. The theater consultant will have a broad range of experience with different theater types, in different places, with different budgets. S/he has detailed knowledge of theatrical systems and the day-to-day operations of a theater. S/he has detailed knowledge and understanding of the process of designing a theater, allowing them to be your advocate. Of all members of the design team, the theater consultant will understand that a "strike" is not a labor stoppage and a "cyc" is not a psych.

When is the best time to hire a theater consultant? Engaging the theater consultant at the initiation of a project will allow them to bring their experience and expertise to bear as you decide the who, what, where, when and why of your theater. Often, however, the theater consultant may not be brought on board until schematic design is complete and sometimes later. Sometimes theater consultants are not involved at all – and we have all worked in those theaters. As with the selection of the architect, your choice of theater consultant should "feel right".

Selecting the Acoustician

Outside of dedicated concert halls the contributions made by the acoustician are often little understood. Their work is not visible in the finished theater and their advice may seem counter-intuitive at times. Their value is in what is heard and, more importantly, what is not heard. Acoustic criteria and requirements for theaters are unique and can increase the cost of the mechanical systems and may be unfamiliar to the engineers. To turn an aphorism on its head, "unfamiliarity can breed contempt". The acoustician, however, is an integral member of the design team and one whose contributions have a direct impact on the success of the theater.

Broadly speaking the work of the acoustician falls into two areas: room shaping and noise control. Working with the architect and theater consultant, the acoustician guides the overall shape of the audience chamber as well as details such as the profile of the balcony face and the shape of the ceiling. Reverberation times and criteria for interior room finishes are specified to insure that appropriate surfaces are sound reflective or sound absorptive. Reflector panels suspended from the ceiling or mounted to the side/rear walls are also in their purview. In short, the acoustician insures that the aural environment, for the audience will be suitable for the spoken word, un-amplified music and amplified music.

We have all attended performances where, during a dramatic pause, the hum and whoosh of the air conditioning is heard; or the sound of running water and passing traffic intrudes. When you hear these things it likely means that there was no acoustician involved in the design of the theater or that their advice was ignored. Noise control is the process of preventing unwanted air-borne and vibration-borne sound from entering the theater. The reverse, preventing sound from exiting the theater, is also true. At the beginning of a project the acoustician will establish noise criteria (NC) to determine the acceptable amount of outside noise in the theater. Based upon the anticipated program of events the criteria will range from NC-0 (silent) for a concert hall, to NC-30 for a school auditorium. As a point of reference, the criteria for an office range between NC-35 and NC-40. The noise criteria will impact the size of air handlers, grilles, ducts and air velocity (within the ducts) as well as the materials and construction methods used for interior and exterior walls and roofs.

Selecting an acoustician you trust and feel comfortable with is especially important as their work is beyond the experience of most people and is not illustrated in photographs or drawings. As with the theater consultant and architect, telephone calls to previous clients and a personal connection are the way to go.

RFQs

A Request For Qualifications is a solicitation to architects who may be interested in designing your theater. RFQs can be long or short but should be designed to solicit detailed information, such as: history of the firm, principals of the firm, specific experience in the design of theaters, experience in your geographical area, approach to design and working with clients, current workload and interest in the project. It generally does not ask the respondents for a fee.

If you have done your homework, the writing of an RFQ is very straightforward and can provide a keen insight into the architectural firms you may wish to hire. Ask for contact information for relevant completed projects and those still under design/construction. Call those references and ask the hard questions. What was it like working with such-and-such architect? Would you hire them again? Why/why not? Did they listen? Did they follow through?

RFQ
Project Name   Auditorium/Theater Consulting
Owner   Consolidated School District
Location   Wilmington, DE
Zip Code   12345
County   Castle
Sector   State/Municipal
Contact Name   Superintendent   Phone (888) 123-4567
Submittal Date   12/29/2004
Guide Ref Num   257 1257 – 11/19/2004

The Consolidated School District is seeking proposals from individuals and/or firms interested in providing auditorium/theater consulting services to the District regarding the School of the Arts auditorium/theater in Wilmington, DE. The scope of work will include the following: Review of the existing facility from an acoustical, audio-visual and technical theater perspective. Meetings with School of the Arts staff to determine their educational program needs with regard to this facility. Recommendations of renovations that will meet the educational requirements and provide a high quality multi-use performing arts space. Included will be preliminary budget information and recommendations for implementation based upon priority. Responses to the RFP should include the following information: Letter of interest (required), Standard GSA Forms 254 and 255 (required). Additional materials as deemed appropriate (optional). Selection criteria will include, but not be limited to: Experience and reputation. Expertise in auditorium/theater renovation programming and design. Capacity to meet requirements (size, financial condition, etc). Location (geographic). Demonstrated ability in similar auditorium/theater consulting projects. Familiarity with public works, especially educational facility design and renovation. Submissions must be received by 4:00 p.m. on Wednesday, December 29, 2004 at the following address: Consolidated School District Major Capital Improvement Program Headquarters. A paper screening, followed by interviews of finalists will be conducted. Questions can be addressed to the Program Administrator.

This item applies to the following Categories and/or locations.
Categories   A/E-Buildings, A/E-Educational Facilities

Figure 5: Sample RFQ

CITY OF ROCKFORD, ILLINOIS
425 EAST STATE STREET
61104

DOUGLAS P. SCOTT
MAYOR

ANDRES SAMMUL
FINANCE DIRECTOR

REQUEST FOR PROPOSALS
RFP No.: 105-M-002

Coronado Theatre Request for Proposals for Management, Operational, and Programming Review

Issued: 1/5/05

Name of Bidding Firm_____

Address:_____City:_____State____Zip_____

Phone:_____Fax:_____

RFP Opening Time and Date: **11:00 a.m., Local Time, Thursday, February 3, 2005**

ABOUT THIS DOCUMENT
This document is a Request for Proposal. Competitive sealed proposals will be evaluated based on criteria formulated around the important features of a product or service including but not limited to, the contractor's experience, qualifications, time required for completing the work, and the fees to be charged. Price may not be determinative in the issuance of a contract for award. Those specific criteria that will be used and considered in evaluation for award are set forth in this document. **The City of Rockford reserves the right to select, and subsequently recommend for award, the proposed equipment or service which best meets its required needs, quality levels, and budget constraints.**

PLEASE MARK THE RETURN SEALED ENVELOPE:
1.   Proposal Opening Date and Time
2.   Title of job
3.   RFP Number

RETURN PROPOSALS TO:
City of Rockford
Central Services Manager
425 East State Street , 4th Floor
Rockford, Illinois 61104
Telephone: (815) 987-5560
PROPOSALS SUBMITTED BY FACSIMILE OR E-MAIL WILL NOT BE ACCEPTED

PROPOSAL RESULTS:
Proposal results may be obtained by telephone at (815) 987-5560; or by fax at (815) 987-5562.

Phone (815) 987-5560
Fax   (815) 987-5562

An Equal Opportunity Employer

TDD # (815) 987-5718

Figure 6: Sample RFP.

Did the project come in on budget? Are the users happy with the finished building?

There are some architectural firms that are pleasant to work with but do not provide an elegant, functional design. There are others who are a pain to work with but provide their clients with wonderful buildings. There are some firms who design great theaters that are always over-budget. Some design theaters that are expensive to operate. Some charge low fees: some charge high fees. You get the picture. The important thing is to be able to assess a firm's abilities and whether you would want to work with them. This consideration will allow you narrow the field and create a short-list of firms who will be sent an RFP.

Interviews

Often a short-list of three to architects will be invited to make a presentation. This may occur after submission of a proposal or before. During their presentation the architect will demonstrate their experience and expertise and why they feel that they are the firm you should select. The presentation may include anything from boards with simple illustrations and photographs to elaborate PowerPoint presentations.

The presentation should allow a good amount of time for questions and answers. This is where you will get a sense of the individual players and their personalities. Do they listen? Do they answer your questions? Are they open to suggestions? As we discussed earlier, the selection of the architect is art as well as science and you should not have to talk yourself into the virtues of a particular firm. If it doesn't feel right, then it probably isn't.

Often interviews are held back-to-back over the course of one or two days. This concentrated activity can be very stressful. You and your colleagues will be presented with a tremendous amount of information in a very short period of time. It is important to schedule time for reflection and discussion immediately after each presentation without having to worry about the next one. As well, the selection group should have an opportunity to "sleep on" what they have heard and have subsequent meetings. I am always puzzled by the great sense of urgency that often accompanies the selection process. You will be selecting a firm to be responsible for your theater; for spending your money; and with whom you will be spending several years.

Why not invest a little time?

RFPs

A Request For Proposal is a solicitation to architects for a fee to design your theater. It typically follows the RFQ but some projects will only issue an RFP. It should be very specific in describing the facility, its intended uses and the responsibilities of the architect. Any information available, such as feasibility studies, ad hoc building committee reports, etc. should be made available. Often, a pre-proposal meeting is held to provide detailed information and to answer questions. The more information the architects have, the better and more accurately they can prepare their proposals. Any state or municipal requirements should also be included. Typical requirements include: professional liability insurance, general liability insurance, EEO statements, non-collusion statements, submission of standard government forms, financial statements, stage agency registrations, etc.

Submission of proposal is always by a certain time on a certain date and timely delivery is the responsibility of the proposers. Proposals are opened at the specified time and, for state and municipal projects, in public. If law requires selection of the low proposal, then the game is over then and there (except for confirmation that the proposal meets all requirements of the RFP). If this is not the case, the proposals are ranked by qualifications. Negotiations with the top ranked firm are entered into and, if successful, that firm is hired. If negotiations fail, then the second ranked firm is contacted.

4 TYPES OF CONSTRUCTION

If you build it they will come

Whether your theater is new construction, renovation or a historic restoration, there will be many common issues. Budget, schedule, financing, loading facilities, theatrical systems, lobby, seating and sightlines are some of the issues that are addressed in the construction of all theaters. How these common issues are addressed is what can vary between construction types. A historic restoration of a land-marked theater may limit options. There may be different financing available depending upon the construction type. Each construction scenario will also have its own unique issues.

The 1980s renovation of the 55th Street Dance Theater/City Center, in New York City, required negotiations with the developer of the adjacent property to allow a stage right wing in what would be a basement of a proposed luxury residential building. These negotiations involved sale of the theater's "air rights" to the developer. Once the real estate issues were dealt with, there was a structural design problem of how to support an entire new building over the new wing space that, of course, wanted to be clear of obstructions. The resolution of this problem, due to a variety and combination of circumstances,

Figure 7: 55th Street Dance Theater.

was to have columns in the new wing, but is was better than no wing at all (the locking rail had been six feet off-stage) and having a line of stagehands against the locking rail to intercept ballerinas as they leapt into the wings.

Design-Bid-Construction

The traditional method is Design-Bid-Construction. The architect is hired and completes all design work before the project is put out to bid (to contractors).

The major advantage to this approach is that it allows time to: select an architect, work with the client and user groups to develop a consensus about all design aspects and to prepare complete and integrated bid documents (i.e. drawings and specifications). Some states and municipalities require this method to be employed for all public projects. A major disadvantage of the traditional method is when the project must, by law, be awarded to the lowest bidder regardless of their qualifications. This scenario, at the least, can create additional stress for all involved parties and, at the worst, can result in a poorly constructed facility that costs more than the original highest bid.

Fast-Track

This approach became popular in the 1980s. A "fast-track" project will start construction before completion of the final design. For example, a parking garage located under the theater will be built before completion of the balance of the facility design. This overlapping of design and construction is intended to reduce the time required for completion of the project. This can be advantageous when project funding is contingent upon commencement of construction by a certain date. It is also helpful if construction costs are rising rapidly or if there are other time constraints. The disadvantages are: reduced time for design, difficulty in modifying the design (after construction has started), additional required coordination and the increased chance of change orders and other cost overruns.

Design/Build

Design/Build can combine the best of both Design-Bid-Construction and Fast-Track without the disadvantages of either. Simply put, a general contractor is hired along with the architect and design team and is paid to work with them on the design of the facility. The presence of a general contractor, on the design team, allows a more accurate understanding of the cost implications of the design. For example, a general contractor can offer building details that may be less expensive while still fulfilling the intent of the architect. They also bring an intimate understanding of the availability of qualified labor and the availability of materials. Perhaps the greatest advantage is a contactor with a detailed understanding of the facility and a professional investment, borne of their participation in the design, in the success of the finished facility.

New Construction

New construction is just that; a theater is being built where there was none

The Cicely Tyson School of Performing and Fine Arts will occupy two full blocks in downtown East Orange, NJ (outside of Newark). The 800-seat theater, one of four performance spaces, is a theater with a 25-foot high proscenium opening. The gridiron had been located 62'-6" above the stage to allow a full-stage drop to be flown out of sight; that is, until the architect informed us that the city had a zoning ordinance limiting the stage house to a height of 70'-0". The roof of the stage house is pitched at about 45 degrees with the lowest interior point being 62'-0". The result was that the elevation of the gridiron and rigging steel had to be lowered proportionately and the pipe travel reduced by 10'-0". Fortunately this is made up by the planned use of a proscenium valance, which will typically lower the proscenium opening to 20'-0"

before. All things are possible and there will be no obstructions to creating your ideal theater … well sorta kinda. As a theatrical production is circumscribed by the space it is mounted in, the parcel of land for your theater comes with certain unalterable parameters. Among these are: building height restrictions, required set-backs, utility locations, access to existing roadways, site drainage requirements, etc.

Is the theater being built in an urban environment, in the suburbs or in the country? Each can add its own unique conditions. Building in a city generally means a noisier environment requiring potentially more expensive construction techniques. Urban construction sites are surrounded by existing buildings and required set-backs may force a more vertical design. The suburbs will be quieter, but you may encounter NIMBY-ism. The building committee may not be so excited at the prospect of a construction site next door or the prospect of post-performance traffic jams on their quiet street. The country, or any area without adjacent homes, may still have air traffic overhead and will require more infra-structure. It just goes to show you … it's always something!

Renovation/Addition

Renovations can range from a new coat of paint to a complete gutting of the interior of the theater. A more typical scenario is that as monies become available, the renovation of one of the theatrical systems may occur. The seating will be refurbished or replaced, a new lighting system installed or the rigging rehabilitated. Larger renovations can include a new or expanded stagehouse, with expanded wing space.

Additions to theaters often occur when the original facility is lacking in support space (i.e. dressing room, offices, shops, etc.). The creation of a theater

Figure 8: Benedum Centre.

The Stanley Theater, in Pittsburgh, PA, was built in 1928 for vaudeville and seated over 3,000. A $42 million dollar renovation and expansion, in the 1980s, saw the Stanley reborn as the Benedum Center for the Performing Arts. The Benedum is home to the Pittsburgh Opera, the Pittsburgh Symphony, the Pittsburgh Ballet Theater and the Pittsburgh Musical Theater. The renovation included: reducing the seat count to 2,800, expanding the stagehouse (to create a larger, deeper stage), new wing space and fly space, new paint and plaster-work, new seating, lighting, rigging and sound systems. An annex was built adjacent to the theater that included: dressing rooms, rehearsal rooms, costume shop, wardrobe maintenance and storage and administrative offices.

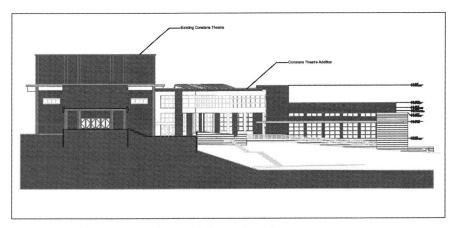

Figure 9 Nadine McGuire Theater & Dance Pavilion.

addition may also be an occasion to create a new performance space.

The Theater Addition at the University of Florida-Gainesville is adjacent and connected to the existing Constans Theater. Prior to the design of this project the University Department of Theater and Dance was scattered across campus with the Constans Theater at one end, dance rehearsal spaces at the opposite end and classrooms in between. The department's primary objective was to gather faculty, staff and facilities to a more centralized location. The new addition includes: a 3,500 square foot studio (i.e. black box) theater, a 2,000 square foot dance performance/rehearsal studio, faculty offices, acting studios, teaching studios and a new costume shop. In addition, the existing scene shop was enlarged as well as the shared loading dock.

Many older theaters have been designated as historical landmarks. This designation is awarded to theaters with significant architectural and historical features. The interior, exterior or both may be landmarked. This offers protection to the facility, but can make renovations more problematic. While the theaters are celebrated for their history, they are still expected to meet current performance standards. Significant changes cannot be implemented unless approved by the historical agency having jurisdiction. Replacing the stage rigging will not likely create any problems. On the other hand, punching a large slot in the ceiling of the auditorium to create a FOH lighting position will raise all sorts of red flags. These are not insurmountable problems, but ones that must be carefully considered during the renovation of any historic theater.

Codes

Regardless of how the theater is to be built or renovated, whether it is new construction or a historic renovation, the prevailing building codes must be adhered to. Building codes describe specific means, methods and materials to be used in the design and construction of any residential or commercial building. The purpose of a building code is to insure that design, construction and safety standards are observed. They provide standards for every conceivable aspect of a building … and in excruciating and often confusing detail. If the building does not meet code, a *certificate of occupancy* (CO or C-of-O) will not be issued. Without a CO, the building cannot be opened.

Codes are usually updated every two years to incorporate the most current changes in building standards, materials and procedures and federal directives (such as ADAAG). The process consists of specified procedures including: review of existing code, proposed changes, meetings of the code writing agency, public review and comment and issuing a revised code. Until recently there were two primary codes adhered to in the United States: Building Officials & Code Administrators (BOCA) and the Uniform Building Code (UBC). Depending upon their geographical location buildings are built according to the code (determined by the state or municipality) as having jurisdiction. Some larger municipalities, such as New York City, have their own building codes (although the NYC Building Code will be phased out in favor of the IBC). Generally speaking, these codes are similar in most respects, the differences being in certain details, procedures, standards and definitions. Before commencing design, it is important that all parties understand which codes will govern as well as the issue date of the code. The most recent issue will not necessarily be the version of the code a project is required to follow.

In the late 1990s code officials acknowledged the benefit of having just one code to be followed by everyone, everywhere and not just in the United States, but globally. The International Building Code (IBC) prepared by the International Code Council is that code and the UBC, BOCA and other municipal codes have been or are in the process of being phased out. Used in conjunction with these, in the United States, are the National Electric Code (NEC) and the National Fire Protection Association Life Safety Code (NFPA 101). Other countries may use the International Electrical Code, International Fire Safety Code or similar that is unique to that country.

Over the past 20-30 years building codes have acknowledged the unique design and use requirements of theaters and the sections addressing *places of assembly* have grown more specific and detailed. This is good and bad. The good part is that many conflicts between code requirements for egress, fire protection, electrical use, ventilation, etc. between typical buildings and theaters have been resolved. Architects and engineers, even without the benefit of a theater consultant, will design better theaters because of the code. The inclusion specific theater-related issues into the code has created more informed code officials. This is very important because, regardless of what the code may say, the local code official has the last word – period – end-of-story.

The bad part is that the resolution does not always make life easier for the design team or the users. The creation of a building code is a long process involving the participation of many persons and organizations that may have conflicting agendas. The validity of any proposed addition or change must be substantiated to the satisfaction of the code writing body. Then it must withstand a year-plus trial of reviews, comments, changes and the politics that invariably play a part in any deliberation of a large body.

Interpretation and satisfaction of the code is the responsibility of the building inspector. In a large municipality; there is often a building department with staff whose job, among other things, is to review and approve plans before construction and to visit the construction site to insure compliance. Building department staff often have experience with a broad range of building types, including theaters (although not necessarily). This can make the design approval process easier (although, again, not necessarily). In smaller cities and towns the building department may contain only one person. In rural areas the building inspector is often the chief of the fire department.

When it comes to building codes, the key word is *interpretation*. Several people can read the same paragraph and report a different finding. An example of code-speak can be found in IBC section 410.3.5, Proscenium Curtain, which reads:

> *The proscenium opening of every stage with a height of greater than 50 feet ... shall be provided with a curtain of approved material or approved water curtain complying with Section 903.3.1.1.*

Well, okay, but the height of what above what? Turning to section 410.2, Definitions, we find that:

> *Stage height shall be measured from the lowest point on the stage floor to the highest point of the roof or floor deck above the stage.*

The stage floor is always level as are the wings, so the low point of the measurement is clear, but is the highest point of the roof the underside or the top? If it is the underside, is it the bottom of the rigging steel or the actual inner roof structure? Is the gridiron regarded as a "floor?" This example is pretty straight forward in so far as to understand section 410.3.5 one only needs to look at one other section (even though it still leaves questions). In other cases one section of a paragraph may refer to another paragraph … that may refer to a table … that may have exceptions … that refer to another graph, etc.

So, we come back to interpretation and more specifically, who has the final say-so and why this is important to the design team and the client. The answer is unambiguous. As noted earlier, the local code official has the last word. If the code official has experience with theaters, then reaching consensus about the interpretation of a code section will be easy. If the code official does not have experience with the unique requirements of theater buildings, achieving consensus may be more problematic. If the code official is a stubborn S.O.B. (Son of a Bitch) then no matter how explicit the code section is or what local precedents you cite, no amount of word parsing may satisfy them. This worst-case scenario will be, at the very least, an aggravation and can end up costing time and money.

Sometimes comments by a building department can focus more on form than substance. During the pre-bid approval process on one project was a comment noting that, in the specification for the fire curtain, the relevant section number of the local code be cited. The specification was resubmitted with the section cited. The specification was returned with the comment that the entire section was required to be cited in-full. This change was made and resubmitted. The building department returned it again saying not to cite the code section in full but only by its number. This type of issue is not one that can be argued and, short of having the inspector's knee-caps broken, there is not much to be done. In this particular case, when the specification was re-written (for a fourth time) this portion was accepted.

Conflicts in code interpretation are not usually as dire as the instances described above. Typically the architect's office has a working relationship with the building department and its staff. Sometimes the design team will include a code consultant who is versed in code-speak and code requirements for theaters. They will offer advice and comment as the design proceeds to minimize and, ideally, prevent any code problems. If conflicts do occur, they can act as the design team's advocate.

Construction Financing

Historically, financing of public performing arts facilities is provided by local, county and state governmental agencies. The rationale is usually contained in a community or economic development plan. Recently colleges and universities alone, or in conjunction with other agencies have financed performing arts facilities. Each venue is unique in its financial requirements and a method that works for one will not necessarily work for another.

A complete description of financing for public assembly spaces is provided in *Developing Sports, Convention and Performing Arts Centers*, 3rd Edition, published by the Urban Land Institute in 2001, by David C. Petersen. For those interested, Mr. Petersen describes many detailed cases of funding for a variety of venues. For the rest of us, it may suffice to sample some of the revenue sources identified in Mr. Petersen's book:

- Increase in excise tax/sales tax for a specified period
- Increased hotel tax rate
- Land appreciation through favorable re-zoning
- Municipal development of parking facilities
- Pari-mutuel tax revenue
- Private contributions
- Rights to concession franchise in other venues
- State general obligation and revenue bonds/appropriations
- Sports lottery
- Tax increment financing
- Use of land at below market cost or at no cost
- Casino taxes
- Center operating revenue
- Commercial building lease revenue
- Development rights on adjacent land
- Facility-specific admission tax

5 THE DESIGN PROCESS

As we discussed in Chapter 2, the design process for building a theater is the same as designing a show … only different. The design of any building proceeds through several discreet phases that have been codified by the American Institute of Architects (AIA) and are generally accepted and followed by the architectural community. Each phase is design to build upon the preceding leading up to a completed facility … at least theoretically.

Because of this step-by-step process, the architect will ask for a sign-off at the completion of each phase. The sign-off is acceptance of the design, up to that point, by you (the client). Once the work of a phase has been signed-off, you cannot ask the architect to go back and re-open earlier decisions – at least not without some additional compensation or increase in the project schedule. In practice, politics and time pressures rarely allow a project to take a step backward. The sign-off is the architect's insurance. It is also your insurance. If you are not happy with the work, say so and do not allow the project design to proceed until you are. This does not have to be an adversarial proposition

As with most things, there is often a gulf between theory and practice. Politics, budget and time constraints often conspire to short-circuit the design process. The design timetable for the Sala São Paolo, a historic restoration of a 1930's train station into a 1,800-seat concert hall, in São Paolo, Brazil was based solely upon completion prior to the upcoming gubernatorial election. There is often nothing that can be done in these situations. As to the Sala São Paolo, which opened in 1998, suffice to say that there were many cost overruns because of the abbreviated design schedule.

Figure 10: Sala São Paolo.

(although sometimes it is) and if you and the design team are working together successfully, then it is just another step in the collaborative process.

A Quick History of Theater Design

It is said that history repeats itself and that those who fail to heed history's lessons are doomed to repeat them. There are, unfortunately, abundant examples of this in theaters around the world. So that we may avoid this prophesy, a short illustrated history of theater design is in order. While not definitive nor comprehensive, we will show some of the highlights of the past 2000 years of Western theater building design.

The basic elements of theater and drama are found in every society no matter how primitive or advanced. They may be seen in the dances and ceremonies of primitive peoples, just as they can be found today in such diverse activities as religious services, political campaigns, parades, sports and children's make-believe. Most of these activities, however, are not intentionally theatrical, even though they may employ theatrical elements.[1] As all art flows from the society and culture that surrounds it, so too does theater and its venues flow. Our examination of theater buildings, perforce confines us to theater as an art form. Theater has existed for tens of thousands of years: around the globe but for our purposes, we will focus on Western Theater.

The first decisive steps toward theater and drama were taken in Greece in the 6th century, BC. [2] In his Poetics, Aristotle cites 'unities of time and place' where he comments that a play will have its action occurring in a single area and that the play will take as long as the action described. (The unity of time is observed today, in the television show '24' where each of 24 episodes describes 1 hour of the drama.) Permanent theater structures, such as the theater at Epidarus, were located to take advantage of landscape, the path of the sun and to facilitate the unities of time and place (facing page).

The Roman Empire borrowed many things from Greek culture including theater buildings. Although relying somewhat more an spectacles ("bread and circuses"), the Romans did have their own indigenous theater. The Greek theater form was maintained, but did not necessarily rely on naturally occurring landscapes to create a seating area (below).

It is often stated that the theater in Western Europe ceased to exist after the fall of Rome in the 6th century A.D., but this assertion must be qualified. During the Middle Ages, official recognition and support of performances were withdrawn, the theater structures ceased to be used, and educated men devoted their energies to a church which sought to stamp out all pagan pastimes including drama. Consequently, the theater existed, if at all, on a much reduced

scale and as a semi-legitimate activity. Actors were anathematized by church councils and Christians were urged to avoid them.[3]

At the same time, the church may be credited with the revival of drama during this period. Although the importance of the Mass discouraged innovation, other services were more amenable to the introduction of drama. The service of the Hours often included playlets. Liturgical dramas described events from the bible and were performed inside the church. Passion plays, due to their scope, were performed outside the church, but remained a church sponsored activity (above).

Long before Medieval drama declined, new conceptions of dramatic form and theatrical production had already taken shape. Beginning during the 14th century, they had spread throughout Europe by 1650 and continued to dominate practice until the 19th century.[4] New scenic practices took great advantage of perspective to create realistic seeming vistas as well as outdoor city spaces and indoor spaces. Magical transformations were created by 'flying' effects, scenic wagons and other devices not unfamiliar to us today. In Italy, designers such as Serlio and Sabatinni created stage spaces within existing buildings as that is where plays were being performed (facing page, top).

William Shakespeare is probably the greatest dramatist of all time. As a playwright, actor and shareholder in acting troupes and theater buildings, he was directly involved in more aspects of the theater than any other writer of his time. He borrowed stories from many sources, but always made them distinctly his own. Typically a number of plots are interwoven, at first proceeding somewhat independently but coming closer together as the denouement

approaches, so that the resolution of one leads to that of the others. He ranges freely through time and place, creating a sense of a fully developed life behind the scenes.[5] Permanent public theaters of the late 16th century, reflected the needs of Shakespeare's plays as well as his contemporaries (overleaf).

Like England, Spain had developed a theater and drama of stature before 1600. The century between 1580 and 1680 was so productive that it is commonly called the Siglo d'Oro or Golden Age of Spanish drama. Although influenced by Classical and Italian ideals, the Spanish theater developed along independent lines.[6] Religious drama, emphasizing the sacraments, became codified as autos sacramentales. Often these were performed in outdoor plazas. Scenic wagons, similar to those used for Passion Plays during the Middle Ages, were often used and abutted to existing buildings. Sometimes these wagons were stacked, one on top of the other and may have had scenic drops suspended from them or between them.

The works of professional playwrights, such as Calderón and Lope de Vega,

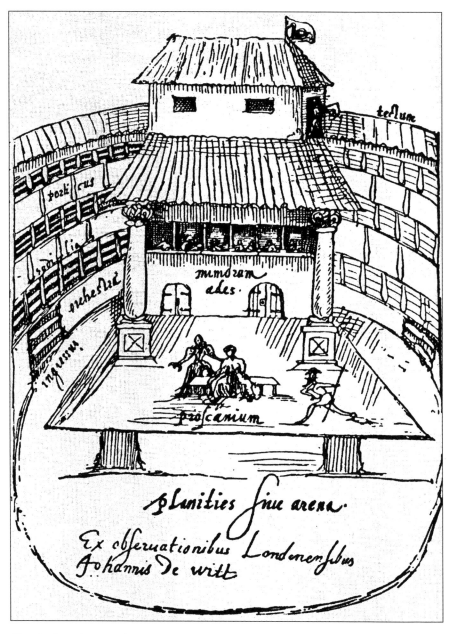

Elizabethan theatre above, Spanish courtyard theatre opposite.

were performed in public theaters, known as corrales (because the theaters were created from existing courtyards) (previous page).

Although the English theater expanded rapidly between 1790 and 1843, the provisions of the Licensing Act denied most companies the rights to present regular drama. Furthermore, the financial depression which followed the Napoleonic Wars made theatrical ventures risky. After 1843, the English theater gradually recovered both financially and artistically. During the last half of the 19th century, pictorial realism reached its apex and actor-managers began to establish unified production as a goal (Theatre Royal, above). [7]

Richard Wagner, Adolph Appia and Edward Gordon Craig were in the vanguard of critical thinking about the nature of theater in the 19th century. In the late 1880s Wagner brought a new awareness of the theater's possibilities.[8] For Wagner the effectiveness of the production depends upon performance as well as upon composition and he argued that the author should supervise every aspect of production in order to synthesize all parts into a Gesamtkunstwerk or 'master art-work'. From these ideas were to stem much of modern theory about the need for a strong director and a unified production (opposite).[9]

Following in Wagner's theoretical footsteps were Adolph Appia and Gordon Craig. Appia advocated the use of three-dimensional scenic units (in lieu of the

two-dimensional scenery which was commonplace) to enhance the performers and blend the horizontal floor with the upright scenery. He emphasized the role of light to fuse all the visual elements into a unified whole. As well, Appia wished to manipulate light in response to shifting moods, emotions and actions as carefully as a musical score.[10] This degree of control only became possible in the early 1970s with the advent of computer controlled lighting systems (above).

Edward Gordon Craig published *The Art of the Theatre* in 1905. It contained many of the ideas set forth by Appia, but it was Craig who published and disseminated them. While Craig and Appia agreed upon many points they differed in others. For Appia, the performer and text were paramount. For

Craig, they were simply elements to be moulded by the director. Craig decried realism and sought to eliminate all non-essential details. His designs often used simple forms that suggested the feel of the play with representing any actual place.[11] The influence of both Appia and Craig still resonates in scenography today (above).

The 20th century started to see critical thinking about the theater translated into the theater buildings themselves. Max Rhinehart presented monumental productions of the Orestia, Julius Caesar and Danton's Death in the Grosses Schauspielhaus (below).

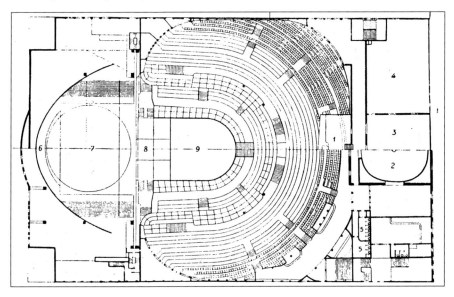

In addition to his plays, Bertolt Brecht is known for his theory of alienation. He wished to make the events taking place on stage to seem sufficiently strange that the audience would question them. To prevent the audience from being lulled into a suspension of disbelief, Brecht had all the mechanics of the theater exposed to view: from stage machinery to lighting to on-stage musicians. In today's black box theaters, we can see Brecht's influence.

The Bauhaus movement of the 1920s sought to break down the traditional barriers between artist and craftsman and to unite architecture, painting, sculpture and other arts into a communal expression.[12] Walter Gropius created a theoretical Total Theater for Irwin Piscator, designed to reflect this. The Total Theater is, perhaps, the ultimate multi-purpose theater. Varied performer/audience relationships and production approaches are possible and the relationship can be altered as part of the production. Projection capabilities are integrated into the theater to created scenic environments that would surround the audience and performers. Although it was never built, it continues to influence theater architecture today (below).

One common element throughout the history of theater is that significant change to theater buildings comes about as a result of the theater artists.

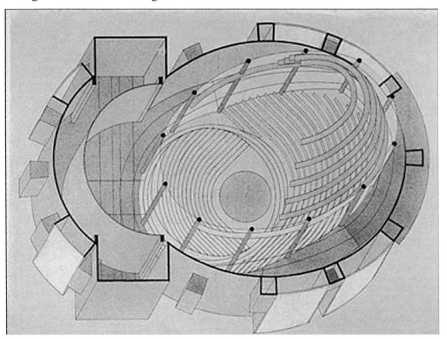

Creativity cannot be imposed from the outside by means of a building, no matter how spiffy the technology. The best theaters, then, should provide possibilities for artists and audiences to use in a variety of ways.

Theater Forms

Over the course of theater history, the relationship between performers and audience has varied considerably. This has been a factor of both 'art' and 'practicality'. Different styles (think: Artaud, Brecht and Brooks) of performance lent themselves to difference arrangements. As well and of necessity audience configurations became more fixed as performances moved into dedicated buildings (The Hôtel de Bourgogne, in Paris, France – built in 1548 – was originally a tennis court). Allowing the flexibility desired by theater artists is one of the primary balancing acts necessary in the design of a new theater. Theater forms (below) shows a variety of performer/audience configurations employed by the University of California in Los Angeles. Although the nature of a black box theater easily permits this variety, it does not mean that it will not be desirable in a more 'fixed' theater space.

There is no 'right' or 'wrong theater form, just as there is there is no ideal theater. Each theater is created in its own context. Today, most theaters fall into the following forms.

Proscenium: where the performers and audience are divided by the proscenium arch. The audience sits on one side and the performance takes place (for the most part) behind or on the other side of the arch.

Thrust: where there may or may not be a proscenium arch and the acting area is injected into the audience with seating on three sides.

Arena or theater-in-the-round: where there is no stage house and the performance area is surrounded on all sides by the audience.

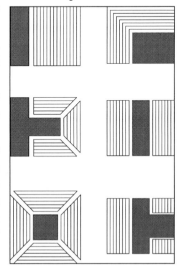

Black Box/environmental/courtyard: where there is no prescribed performance area or seating area. While there may be some permanent seating areas included (say in a balcony surrounding the space) each production may have a unique performer/audience arrangement.

The Paper Trail

The design and construction of a theater is a complex and expensive undertaking that can last several years and will include the participation of hundreds of persons. Choices are discussed and decisions are made – or not made – at all times during the project. As time passes, memories dim and the events leading up to a prior action can be difficult to reconstruct. To maintain the history of the project and to prevent finger-pointing (remember, building a theater involves lots of money) all meetings will have minutes taken. Phone calls will be documented as well as any *ad hoc* discussions. Of course, all correspondence will be cataloged and sketches and drawings saved. Maintaining a paper trail may sound bureaucratic and tedious – and it is, but it is a necessary evil that creates a historical record and ensures that tasks and responsibilities are met.

Even with the best intentions, note-takers make mistakes. Minutes are typically presumed to be correct unless the author is notified. During meetings, take your own notes, read the minutes and make sure they are correct. If there is an error or you feel an item is not taken in proper context, have the author amend the document.

Programming and Pre-design

This phase lays the foundation for the facility by determining uses, spaces, overall size and room adjacencies. Programming includes two primary activities: a space summary and room adjacencies. A space summary lists all required spaces and their net square footage. This is usually presented as a list or spread sheet. Room adjacencies are displayed in a matrix format or diagrammatically (the bubble diagram being the most common).

Pre-design will include locating the facility on the site, vehicular circulation and the general shape and massing of the building.

If members of the design team are located in disparate parts of the country, much communication will take place via email and over the phone. Airfare has become very expensive and so it is in everyone's interest to keep expenses to a minimum. This is fine for information collection and preliminary work but there is no substitute for the "human" connection. Just as production meetings are required for a show, design meetings are required for the design of a theater. In both cases the meetings are not solely for nuts-and-bolts considerations, but also for everyone to get to know each other, knock ideas around, develop consensus and, in short, become the team that will be

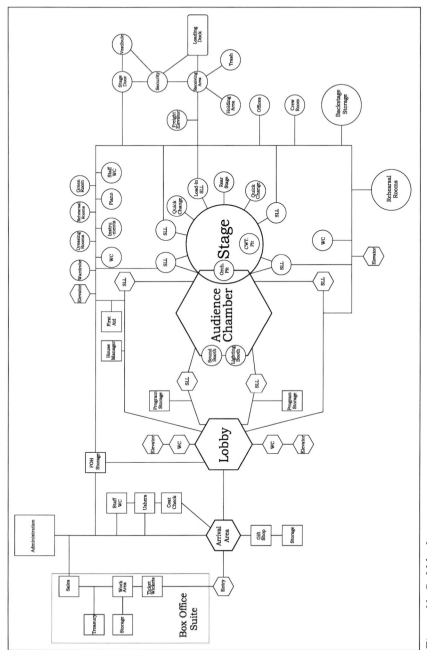

Figure 11: Bubble diagram.

necessary for the successful completion of the theater. There are two very useful and effective activities that you and the design team may elect to do at this point in the project.

The first is to go on a *road trip*. Go visit other theaters of similar size and program to see how they addressed the design of their facility. Identify what was successful and what was, "Oh, my lord – what were they thinking!" For a small project, it may only be necessary to visit a few other theaters nearby. For larger projects (with more time and more money available) travel out-of-state and even to other countries may be appropriate. The administration of Nashville Symphony, whose new concert hall openned in 2007, took their design team on a tour of European concert halls of historic renown.

The second is a design *charette*. An academic exercise performed by architects during their training, a charette is an intensive, roll-up-your-sleeves process where a project is embraced in its entirety over a short period of time to develop the *gestalt* of it. In our context, a charette will bring all the players into the same room with tracing paper, models, black boards, colored pens, coffee, tea, munchies and with lunch brought in to start pulling all the pieces of the design together. The architect may bring some rough drawings and/or

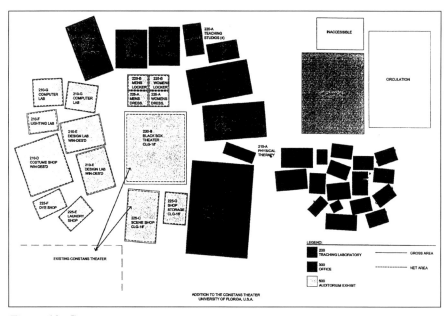

Figure 12: Cut-outs.

simple models of various building components. These pieces can be moved around to evaluate adjacencies and the overall appearance of the building. The charette can last from one to three days depending upon the complexity of the project and how well everyone gets along. There are no hard and fast rules. A road trip is not a prerequisite to conducting a design charette but you may easily imagine how useful it can be.

Schematic Design

This phase takes the pre-design, space program and room adjacency, developed in the previous phase, and translates them into scaled plans and sections. At this point the building design is still very pliable. It is a time for you and the design team to put yourselves in the building and to imagine the day-to-day activities and how they will be accomplished. Identification of problems and conflicts are to be expected and encouraged. Better to know about them, at this early stage, than later on when it will be more difficult to address.

This phase will see the beginnings of coordination between the various building disciplines. Routing of conduits, plumbing, sprinklers and air ducts will be prepared by the engineers. The theater consultant will begin to locate components of the theatrical systems and describe their architectural, structural, electrical and mechanical requirements to the design team. Seating

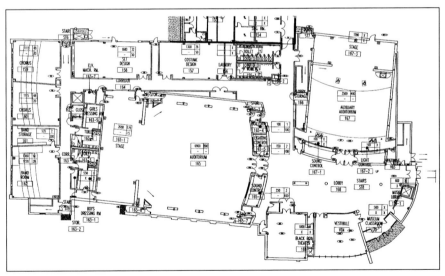

Figure 13: Cicely Tyson Fine & Perfoming Arts School.

and sightlines will be developed and evaluated along with public and technical circulation. The acoustician will develop noise criteria appropriate for the program of the facility and assist the design team to meet it. They will also develop room finishes and determine which surfaces need to be hard (reflective) or soft (absorptive). The acoustician will describe adjustable acoustic features, such as draperies, banners and panels that may be required to meet the room's program.

Design Development

Design development is where the problems identified during schematic design are resolved and final decisions are made. This is where the theater takes its real shape. Plans, sections and elevations of all spaces are prepared. Exterior elevations are developed and appropriate architectural and engineering details are developed. Room finishes and lighting plans (Reflected Ceiling Plans) are created. Structural, electrical and mechanical loads are finalized, along with

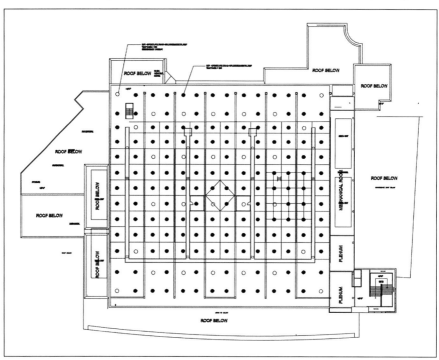

Figure 14: Reflected Ceiling Plan.

their pathways through the building. All aspects of the building are identified and, ideally, resolved.

The theater consultant and acoustician will review the work of the design team to make sure that the day-to-day function of the theater is unimpaired and that the architect and engineers have properly accommodated the theatrical and acoustic systems.

Construction Documents

The Construction Documents describe, in drawings and written specifications, all aspects of the theater. Construction documents (CDs) for a single theater can include hundreds of drawings and thousands of pages of specifications. This is where the architect and design team put it on-the-line. If something is unclear or missed, the bidders will not include it in their bids. CDs prepared by the theater consultant include all theatrical systems and moveable acoustic systems. The acoustician's recommendations are typically folded into the electrical and mechanical specifications.

Specifications are arranged by building trades into divisions organized in a format created by the Construction Specification Institute. This standardized CSI format is used for all building types.

Division 1	General Requirements
Division 2	Site work
Division 3	Concrete
Division 4	Masonry
Division 5	Metals
Division 6	Wood and Plastic
Division 7	Thermal and Moisture Protection
Division 8	Doors and Windows
Division 9	Finishes
Division 10	Specialties
Division 11	Equipment
Division 12	Furnishing
Division 13	Special Construction
Division 14	Conveying Systems
Division 15	Mechanical
Division 16	Electrical

Figure 15: CSI division titles.

These divisions adequately cover general construction, but the needs of a theater can often fall between the cracks. In an effort to incorporate theatrical equipment and systems, in a clear and consistent manner, new sub-divisions have been proposed. Stage lighting consoles and accessories, for example, currently included in division 16 would be moved to division 11, as would sound system equipment. Stage platforms would be specifically identified in division 12. The intent of these changes is to provide more detailed information to contractors who may not have experience in the construction of theaters. As of this writing, these proposed changes have not yet been formally accepted.

All construction documents must be prepared by professional architects and engineers licensed to practice in a given state. This is evidenced on all drawings by a stamp or seal issued to them. Although some theater consultants have licensed engineers on staff, the theatrical systems and equipment CDs are usually covered by the architect's stamp.

Figure 16: Architect's stamp.

Bidding

When the contract documents are complete, they are sent out for bid (in Canada and other countries this process is known as tender). Contractors have a fixed period of time to respond. A pre-bid meeting for interested parties may be held. Sometimes attendance is mandatory and sometimes not. Required attendance can be a good way to winnow the field. If a bidder is willing to spend their own money to attend, it is a good indicator of their interest. Questions raised by bidders, and the answers, should be circulated to all bidders. If there is a change in the bid documents or the bid schedule, an addendum to the bid is issued. There may be several addenda issued depending upon the nature of the project.

Bids can be organized in several ways. A Lump-Sum bid is made by a general contractor and includes all sub-contractors, labor, material, equipment and whatever else may be required to complete the facility. Multiple-Bids are carried out under the aegis of a Construction Manager (CM) who bids each sub-contract separately. The CM manages the entire project and is responsible for the work of all the sub-contractors required to complete the facility. Guaranteed Maximum Price (GMP) is usually employed in a design/build situation. As the builder is a participant in the design process and familiar with the building, they will have enough information to submit a fixed price that will not be exceeded. Each method has its supporters and detractors but choice of which method is the hands of the owner and members of the design team do not participate in the decision.

Sometimes the theatrical systems (lighting, rigging, sound, seating, etc.) are purchased directly by the owner. Sometimes the lighting and sound will be purchased under the electrical contract (Division 16-Electrical). Sometimes the seating and rigging is purchased under the general contract (Division 12-Specialties). Each option has its pros and cons and these will be discussed later. Regardless of how the theatrical systems are bid, the vendors for this specialized equipment should be identified. This is usually accomplished in each system specification section written by the theater consultant, where "listed", "acceptable" or "pre-qualified" vendors are described. This process

---

Addendum No.2
November 10, 2004

Request for Proposals for Prime Consultant Services and Request for Qualifications for Subconsultant Services relating to Renaissance Square Joint Development Project, City of Rochester, Monroe County, New York

2-1. Page 20, Section IV A, Pre-Submittal Conference, delete the first sentence of the paragraph which begins "A pre-submittal conference will be held...." and replace it with the following: "A pre-submittal conference will be held for this RFP/RFQ at the SUNY Brockport MetroCenter, 55 St. Paul Street, Rochester, NY 14604, on November 18, 2004 at 10:00 AM."

2-2. Page 21, Section IV B, Submission Requirements, in the second paragraph which begins "Submittals should provide..." change the second sentence to require eight (8) copies of qualification statements for Subconsultant contracts.

2-3. Page 24, Section V A, Qualifications and Experience of the Project Team, delete the first paragraph and the first three bullets. Remove the fourth bullet to make this the first paragraph of the section. Add under this new paragraph with begins, "In evaluating the Prime Consultant proposals..." a new bullet as follows: "Experience working as part of a complex consultant team"

Figure 17: Addendum.

has two principal advantages: it lets a contractor bidding the project know who to call, as they may never have bid a theater project before. It also guarantees an apples-to-apples comparison of bids. The contractor is required to bid one of the identified theatrical vendors – even if they wish to propose an un-listed vendor as an alternate.

As with the RFP, submission of bids is always by a certain time on a certain date and timely delivery is the responsibility of the bidder. Bids are opened at the specified time and, for state and municipal projects, in public. If law requires selection of the low bid, then the game is over then and there (except for confirmation that the proposal meets all requirements of the bid). If this is not the case, the bids are ranked by qualifications and inclusion of all of the bid requirements. Negotiation with the top ranked firm is begun and, if successful, that firm is hired. If negotiations fail, then the second ranked firm is contacted.

Value Engineering

A method of analysis that became popular in the 1980's, value engineering is a tool used to save money. The principle is to find ways to complete a project for less money while retaining its desired "value". Every element in the building is assigned a relative value. Those items deemed of great value are retained: those deemed of lesser value are modified or eliminated. Seems to be a good idea – helps keep priorities in order – keeps client and design team on the same page – and purports to increase value while decreasing costs – but does it?

In the 1966 movie Gambit, Michael Caine's character has a plan to pull off a major robbery and needs Shirley McCaine's character as a gambit and window dressing for his plan to succeed. The opening of the movie shows the plan as a dream sequence where everything goes exactly according to plan. Then the film shows us the plan's actual execution where, of course, everything goes wrong. I believe this is often what happens when value engineering is applied to performing arts facilities. It's not that I believe the process is flawed, but that it is often applied at inappropriate times with unrealistic expectations.

Although the cost of a design should be monitored at each design phase, it often happens that bids come in significantly over budget. This can be the result of poor budget accounting during design, wishful thinking on the part of the client and design team, an unforeseen jump in labor or material costs or a malfunctioning crystal ball. Whatever the reason, there is almost never additional funding available and so the design team must find ways to reduce the cost of the facility.

The knight-in-shining-armor most often called upon is value engineering, the process where all aspects of the theater are evaluated to ascertain their value. Those items deemed of great value are retained: those deemed of lesser value are modified or eliminated. The only problem is that everyone has their own idea of what is valuable to a theater. Substituting gypsum board for plaster will not likely be a problem for anyone. Re-design of the architect's cherished lobby window wall, will be a disappointment but after the theater is built, no one will ever know. Deleting 25% of the stage lighting circuits and 50% of the counterweight rigging sets can seriously handicap the theater over the course of its entire existence. It may seem far-fetched but in these situations it is often the theatrical systems, essential to the function of the facility, that are asked to suffer significant cuts.

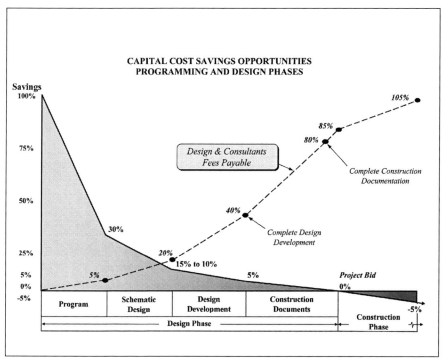

Figure 18: Value engineering opportunities.

The client/owner is the ultimate arbiter of the value engineering process, although the work of creating value engineering choices is delegated to the architect. Sometimes the client elects to bring in an outside party to oversee the process. The rationale in hiring an outside firm is that the architect and design team may be too emotionally invested and another firm will be able to review the project with clear eyes. It also implies that all the parties selected to create the facility (architect, design team, facility manager and owner) have failed in some regard and/or are not professional enough.

In my experience, this reasoning is flawed. Usually a construction management firm is engaged and charged with reducing the cost of the facility to the monies available … period. Despite the best of intentions, they can have no understanding of the history of the project, consensus that has been built or the relationships, professional and social, which have accrued. They are often granted carte blanche and the architect and design team are expected to accede a year or more's work to a relative stranger with minimal time allotted and, most often, no additional fee. You may imagine the unpleasant climate this creates. In fact, it can poison the entire construction process.

Aside from licking old wounds, I am writing this as a cautionary tale to help make performing arts facilities the best they can be. Keep track of project costs at all times during the design process. A cost consultant can be a very valuable member of you team in this regard. If the project is over-budget at any point in the design, it should be addressed then. The earlier a budget problem is identified the easier it will be to remedy and the less it will cost. As the design proceeds through construction documentation, budget problems become increasing difficult to remedy and will increase in cost. If you attempt to implement value engineering at this late stage, you will end up with less building for the money. To paraphrase Yoda, the Jedi master, "Be afraid … be very afraid!"

Design Around the World

The tasks described in the previous chapters should be applied to the design of any theater in any part of the world. The formal design phases described at the beginning of this chapter are based upon practice in the United States and Canada. As discussed, each design phase leads to the next and each subsequent phase is more detailed leading, finally, to the bid drawings. Other countries, however, may follow a different sequence of design work leading to the bid drawings. The following sections, while not a comprehensive examination of global procedures, will give a general idea of the most common design procedures.

Mexico, South America and Spain

These countries all follow the design stages listed below.

Estudio (study) is the programming and pre-design phase where the scope of the work is determined.

Ante Proyecto (literally "before the project") is equivalent to the schematic design phase where the shape and form of the building are laid out.

Proyecto Basico (basic project) is akin to the design development design phase where the final shape and form of the building are confirmed and major technical issues are resolved. Many times the project will be bid-based upon the work completed in the Proyecto Basico, with minimal written specifications. The process then follows more of a design/build format. It is understood by all parties that the drawings do not completely detail all aspects of the building (as Construction Documents would) and that a construction budget contingency will be allowed to cover additional construction costs that may arise. In Brazil the contingency may be as high as 50%, but the actual amount varies from country to country and from project to project.

Proyecto Executivo or Proyecto Legal ("Executive" or "Legal" Project) provides detailed drawings and specifications similar to those prepared during the Construction Document phase.

United Kingdom and Australia

The Royal Institute of British Architects (RIBA) Standard Form of Agreement (SFA/99, updated 2004) and Royal Australian Institute of Architects (RAIA) each divide the design of a theater into a number of distinct project milestones known as Work Stages. For a complex building, such as a theater, additional schedules may be added to describe the tasks of each Work Stage in greater detail.

United Kingdom

Feasibility

- A. Appraisal – Identification of Client's requirements and of possible constraints on development. Preparation of studies to enable the Client to decide whether to proceed and to select the probable procurement method.
- B. Strategic Brief – Preparation of brief confirming key requirements and constraints. Identification of procedures, organizational structure and range of Consultants and others to be engaged for the Project.

Pre-construction

C.   Outline Proposals – Development of the Strategic Brief into a full Project Brief. Preparation of outline proposals and review of procurement route.

D.   Detail Proposals – completion of development of the Project Brief and preparation of detailed proposals. Application for planning approval.

E.   Final Proposals – Preparation of final proposals for the Project sufficient for coordination of all components and elements of the Project.

F.   Product Information – Preparation of production information in sufficient detail to enable a tender to be obtained. Application for statutory approvals.

G.   Tender Documentation – Preparation and collation of tender documentation in sufficient detail to enable a tender to be obtained for the construction of the project.

H.   Tender Action – Identification and evaluation of potential contractors and/or specialists for the construction of the Project. Obtaining and appraising tenders and submission of recommendations to the Client

Construction

I.   Mobilization – Letting the building contract, appointing the contractor and issuing of production information. Arranging of site handover to contractor.

J.   To Practical Completion – Administration of the building contract up to and including practical completion. Provision of additional information to contractor as and when required.

K.   After Practical Completion – Making final inspections and settling of the final account.

Australia
Australian practice is similar, in most respects, to North America.

European Union
The European Union has merged the economies of the major European countries into one and also seeks to unify common professions and activities. In late 2005 the European Union and the AIA signed a reciprocal agreement allowing US professional architects, in practice for a specified number of years, to practice in Europe and *vice versa*. As yet, however, there is no "standard form of agreement" for the European Union and each country follows its own laws, rules of practice and customs.

France

Early design phases in France more or less run parallel to US practice. Plan-Conceptuel (ESQ) is the equivalent of programming and pre-design. Avant-Projet Sommaire (APS) corresponds to Schematic Design and Avant-Projet Détaille (APD) relates to Design Development. Typically Dossier de Consultation des Entreprises (DCE) follows, which is similar to Construction Documents, but not quite. DCE will provide sufficient information to allow the project to be bid but it is expected that final design solutions and details will be developed with the selected building contractors – a sort of design/build arrangement. The design may contain more information than a Proyecto Basico, but less than Construction Documents. Sometimes an Exécution de la Conception (EXE) phase will follow the Avant-Projet Détaillé where, with or without contractors, Construction Document level drawings and specifications are prepared. Bidding, construction and final inspections follow.

Belgium

Belgium follows a two-stage process. Avant-Projet encompasses Schematic Design and Design Development. Projet covers Constructions Documents including complete drawings and specifications.

Germany

Germany is similar to North American practice with Schematisches Design (SD), Designentwicklung (DD) and Bauakten (CD).

Asia

India, China, Japan, Korea and the smaller countries of Asia each have a rich and unique theater culture that is as old as western theater (and in some cases older). The Noh Theater and Kabuki Theater each have their own theatrical conventions and theater building designs. The Japanese Bunraku Theater employs large dolls that are manipulated by puppeteers dressed completely in black. As the staging for these forms grew more complex, in the early 18th century, they led to the invention of stage machinery which has since been adopted throughout the world. In 1727, elevator traps were introduced to raise scenery through the floor, and after 1757 they were used to create different stage floor levels. In 1758 the revolving stage (known today as a "turn-table") was invented.[1]

Figure 19: Kabuki Theater.

While provisions for ancient theater forms are accommodated in new theater buildings constructed in Asia today, those theaters generally follow western forms as well as a western design approach.

[1] Brocket, Oscar History of the Theatre.1968. Allyn and Bacon. p. 1

[2] Brocket, Oscar History of the Theatre.1968. Allyn and Bacon. p. 9

[3] Brocket, Oscar History of the Theatre.1968. Allyn and Bacon. p. 81, 82

[4] Brocket, Oscar History of the Theatre.1968. Allyn and Bacon. p. 125

[5] Brocket, Oscar History of the Theatre.1968. Allyn and Bacon. p. 166

[6] Brocket, Oscar History of the Theatre.1968. Allyn and Bacon. p. 196

[7] Brocket, Oscar History of the Theatre.1968. Allyn and Bacon. p. 434

[8] Brocket, Oscar History of the Theatre.1968. Allyn and Bacon. p. 400

[9] Brocket, Oscar History of the Theatre.1968. Allyn and Bacon. p. 418

[10] Brocket, Oscar History of the Theatre.1968. Allyn and Bacon. p. 567

[11] Brocket, Oscar History of the Theatre.1968. Allyn and Bacon. p.568

[12] Brocket, Oscar History of the Theatre.1968. Allyn and Bacon. p.598

6 BUILDING THE THEATER

Construction

The successful bidder is charged with construction of the facility for the bid/negotiated price and within the time-frame specified. Usually the general contractor's overall work, and that of their sub-consultants, is overseen by the architect with the engineers and other consultants observing the work of their specific disciplines. Sometimes a Construction Manager is hired to supervise and monitor the construction. Their task is to keep the project on schedule, address unforeseen field conditions, resolve questions or perceived conflicts within the construction documents, authorize partial payments to the contractors and take care of any

Figure 20: Nadine McGuire Pavilion during construction.

loose ends. Participation of a construction manager does not change the responsibility of the architect and design team to monitor the execution of the design, but relieves them of certain mundane details of the process.

RFIs

A Request For Information is issued by a contractor seeking missing information, clarification of information given or resolution of an apparent conflict within the drawings and/or between the drawings and the specification. The RFI is directed to the consultant responsible for the area of work cited in the RFI. Sometimes an RFI is only looking for an answer to the contractor's question. Sometimes, it is the first step in a contractor's search for a change order. The consultant's response must be carefully considered.

A.D. MORGAN
CORPORATION

REQUEST FOR INFORMATION

From:	The A.D. Morgan Corporation P.O. Box 14365 Gainesville, FL 32604	RFI No.:	299
To:	Theatre Design, Inc. 3 Short Street Cold Spring, New York 10516	Date:	April 3, 2004
Project:	Constans Theatre Addition	Pages:	2
ATTN:	Michael Mell		
XC:	Gabriel Jaroslavsky		

We request an interpretation or clarification consistent with the Contract Documents of the subject below. Please advise as soon as possible by returning a completed copy of this form to the undersigned.

Subject: Constans Theatre Conduit System

Ref: Theatre Sound

1   Boxes C181, C182 (OG06), C182 (CG10), C183 and C184 do not have the proper conduits installed to them. Boxes noted per SC Docs, not electrical plans.

We propose the following modifications to allow the correct infrastructure.

C181 – not required by SC Docs. Will add a plate to this box and leave for future use.
C182 (OG06) – Relocate to the east 10 feet and install required conduits
C182 (OG10) – Reinstall with correct conduits on North wall of this room.
C183 – Add required conduits to this box.
C184 - Add conduits, but surface mount on the wall in the Loding Dock/ Shop Area.

Please advise us how we will proceed.

Signed: A. D. Morgan   Date: March 22, 2004

COMMENTS
APR 13 2004
THEATER DESIGN INC
#0112

718 N. Renzilie Dr. Tampa, FL 33609 ■ Fax (813) 831-9860 ■ (813) 532-3033 ■ CRC044502 ■ 2112 W. New Haven Ave ■ Fax (407) 727-7735 ■ (407) 728-2611

Figure 21: RFI.

Change Orders

Ideally the construction documents include every system, every building method, every material and detail required for construction. In reality, there can be unintentional omissions, contradictions between drawing and specification and unforeseen conditions in the field that are unknown at the time of bid. If any of these conditions require additional time, labor or materials, the contractor

HARVEY CONSTRUCTION
CORPORATION OF NEW HAMPSHIRE

Ten Harvey Road ● Bedford, New Hampshire 03110-6805 ● TEL: 603-624-4600 ● FAX: 603-668-0389

March 26, 2001

Mr. Ronald D. Williams
SMRT
144 Fore Street
PO Box 618
Portland, Maine 04104

Reference: Falmouth High School
              Falmouth, Maine

Dear Ron,

The electrical contractor for the aforementioned project has reviewed the Barbizon Lighting scope, shop drawings and has had coordination meetings at the job site. This review has created the follow additional costs.

Falmouth Electric, Inc. $6,181.00
HCCNH mark up $ 618.00
       Total $6,799.00

Please review and advise. If acceptable a formal change proposal will be processed.

Sincerely,

Harvey Construction Corporation of New Hampshire

Paula M. Foss
Project Manager

Figure 22: Change Order.

will ask for a Change Order (also known as an extra). This is additional money to compete tasks that were not included in their bid. A colleague once told me that, "… some contractors make their money by doing their job … and some make their money by not". Change Orders can be the vehicle whereby a contractor, who has deliberately or unintentionally under-estimated their costs, will make up for it. It is the responsibility of the Construction Manager or Architect to determine the validity of any Change Order and then make a recommendation to the owner to accept it or not.

Project construction budgets usually include a contingency fund ranging from 5-10% for unforeseen conditions. These field conditions are to be expected but in certain instances can be drained very quickly. Sometimes, the contingency fund is eliminated during value engineering. In either case, if a change order is presented and there is no more money, there are only a few choices: negotiate the Change Order by proposing a different method of construction or material; sacrifice something else in exchange; forego the work required by the Change Order or try to convince the contractor that a Change Order is not required because the work is, indeed, covered in the construction documents. People being people, this can sometimes be an acrimonious process.

Shop Drawings

Shop drawings are prepared by each contractor and vendor to describe exactly what they propose to provide and install. Copies of the contract drawings, with the title block changed, are not acceptable. Shop drawings are reviewed by the architect and/or appropriate design team member for correctness and adherence to the spirit of the contract documents. The drawings are then returned to the contractor with a stamp issued by the reviewing consultant.

REVIEWED: the shop drawing is acceptable and fabrication may proceed.

MAKE CORRECTIONS AS NOTED: drawing is acceptable subject to comments made on the drawings. No resubmission of the drawing is required and fabrication may proceed.

REVISE AND RESUBMIT: revise the drawing, as noted, and resubmit for review. Fabrication may not proceed until a subsequent review is accepted.

REJECTED: the items shown in the drawing are completely unsuitable.

Shop drawings represent the last chance to catch any mistakes or omissions. Any changes made after successfully reviewed shop drawings have been returned may result in a change order.

Site Visits

Site visits are made by all of the design team members during the course of construction. They can be made on a scheduled basis or as need arises (such as resolution of a conflict between building trades). The purpose of all site visits is to monitor the construction of the theater and to ensure that the integrity and spirit of the design is followed.

In the construction of all buildings, the trade that is on-site first has first choice as to where they install their equipment. The electrical contractor may see the large empty wall (intended for the counterweight rigging system) as the perfect place to run conduit to the dimmer room. The mechanical contractor may suspend ductwork under the fly gallery, reducing the required clearance for the orchestra shell. Sprinkler pipes may be attached to the lighting catwalk, right in the middle of the zone where the stage lighting fixtures must hang. These circumstances are all taken from actual projects and occurred even though the contract documents identified these areas.

Figure 23: Site visit.

Part of the theater consultant and acoustician's work is to keep an eye out so that the work of all building trades is coordinated and that the installation and operation of the theatrical and acoustic systems is not compromised. An appropriate number of site visits should be included in their fee so that visits can be made on a regular basis. Not only does this allow the theater consultant to catch things; it allows them to develop a rapport with the contractors so that if the contractor notices something awry, they will call the consultant. It also allows for a certain amount of horse trading whereby a contractor may alter some piece of their work at the consultant's request in exchange for modification of something else, without a change order. No change orders are good change orders!

If the theater consultant/acoustician is not contracted for regular visits, it will fall to you to be their eyes and ears. During construction, nothing beats being there and seeing things for yourself.

Systems Inspection and Commissioning

Systems inspections occur when installation of the theatrical systems is substantially complete and obstacles, such as scaffolding and other construction items, have been removed from the stage and seating area. It is a visual inspection of the equipment itself and how it has been installed. Any conflicts with building structure or adjacent items and any incomplete portions will be noted for correction. The stage lighting vendor, for example, will confirm that all stage dimming and control circuits have been checked for continuity and polarity. The contract specification will require that all of the theatrical trades confirm that their systems and equipment have been checked and are ready for commissioning by the theater consultant.

Commissioning of the theatrical systems occurs after successful completion of the inspection and may occur immediately afterward. This is the time to look under the hood and kick the tires. In addition to a detailed visual inspection, all aspects of a theatrical system are checked to confirm that they operate properly and per the design. A load will be placed on all dimmers and the functions of the lighting control console will be demonstrated. The sound system outlets will have appropriate devices plugged in and tested. All of the counterweight rigging sets will be operated. The fire curtain will be lowered. The house curtain will be raised and lowered. All seats will be checked to confirm the quiet operation of the self-rising mechanism. The orchestra pit lift will be raised and lowered several times and obstructions created to demonstrate safety features. Any feature that falls short is noted on a punch list for correction. Minor items, such as absence of labeling will not prevent the theater consultant from accepting the system. If a majority of the counterweight rigging sets do not operate smoothly, a re-inspection will be required.

If pre-qualified theatrical vendors have been selected there will be few problems at this point. After all, that is why the theater consultant proposed them in the first place. If you and your theater consultant have monitored general construction and the installation of the theatrical systems, problems will be addressed as they occur and the system's inspection and commissioning will be successful.

Punch Lists

At substantial completion of the theater, the architect, construction manager, owner and design team will look into every nook and cranny of the building according to their discipline. The result of this tour will be a punch list: a list of items and issues that remain to be resolved before the owner will accept the building. Typically monies are withheld from all contractors and sub-contractors to ensure compliance with punch list items.

On August 5, 2004 we visited the Arlington CSD Elementary and Middle Schools to inspect the stage rigging and stage lighting systems. Our comments are noted below.

Middle School
Stage Rigging
1. Lower main valence sufficiently to mask first lighting batten.
2. Provide locking cover for movie screen control.
3. Complete wiring of movie screen.
4. Re-trim all draperies during 6-month check-up.

Stage Lighting
1. We recommend purchase of a lockable, rolling desk to house the lighting control console and its accessories. Anthrocart is one of several manufacturers of these cabinets.
2. Fourth Phase to provide programming of Entry Stations.

Elementary School
Stage Rigging
1. Move valence as far downstage as possible.
2. Move main curtain to +/- 6" of valence
3. Provide locking cover for movie screen control.
4. Re-trim all draperies during 6-month check-up.

Stage Lighting
1. We recommend purchase of a lockable, rolling desk to house the lighting control console and its accessories. Anthrocart is one of several manufacturers of these cabinets.
2. Fourth Phase to provide programming of Entry Stations.

Figure 24: Punch list.

7 THEATRICAL SYSTEMS AND EQUIPMENT

For many users the theatrical systems and equipment are the end-all and be-all of a theater – the exciting toys, the stuff that makes the magic happen. As you will have realized during reading this book, the theatrical equipment is just one piece of the building, albeit an important one. If all aspects of the theater are not properly addressed, the most wonderful lighting console or mixing board will be meaningless.

There are many texts that discuss the design and function of theatrical systems and equipment. They and your theater consultant should be consulted for unique situations. For our purposes, it will suffice to discuss commonly installed equipment.

How To Buy The Gear

The theater consultant will prepare specifications and drawings to describe the theatrical systems for bid. These documents will describe the intent, as well as the letter, of the design of the systems and will provide a common basis for the bids. How much the equipment costs, however, is the result of how it is bid.

It is common for the stage rigging and fixed seating to be bid in CSI Division 12 – Special Equipment and the stage lighting and sound to be bid in CSI Division 16 – Electrical. The advantage to this arrangement is that the electrical contractor (who bids Division 16) is directly responsible for all coordination and details involved in the installation of the lighting and sound systems. The general contractor (who bids Division 12) is responsible for coordination of the rigging and seating. This scenario precludes any finger-pointing.

The disadvantage is that it is common practice for the general contractor and sub-contractor to mark-up the price of the equipment supplied. In a lump-sum bid, the electrical contractor's mark-up would be 10% and the general contractor's mark-up would be an additional 10%. You will never know what the gear really costs and this can put you in a difficult position if you wish to negotiate a change to the equipment package or if the project is value engineered.

One way to avoid contractor mark-up and to know the exact cost of the equipment is for the owner to purchase the equipment directly. The general contractor and electrical sub-contractor are then assigned those contracts and given additional monies to provide the necessary coordination. The percentage paid to the contractors for coordination, in this scenario, will certainly be less than the 10% + 10%.

So, why not always buy direct and save the mark-up? Significant savings usually occur only in large theatrical installations with several venues. For a high school auditorium or small regional theater, it may not be worth the time or cost for the additional bids. Some projects are only permitted to bid the theatrical systems through Division 12 and 16; it's just the way the purchasing system is set up. (This is often the case with municipal and educational projects.) The best way to purchase the theatrical equipment will vary and each project must be evaluated on its individual requirements.

The Players

Different manufacturers of theatrical systems and equipment employ different levels of response to a bid, depending upon the project location and its size. The principal players are noted below.

Manufacturer or OEM is the company that actually designs and fabricates the equipment.

Dealer is a sales agent for different non-competing manufacturers. Dealers re-sell the equipment and make their profit on the mark-up.

Manufacturer's Rep is a sales agent for a variety of manufacturers who makes a commission on any represented products that are sold in their territory.

Systems Integrator will package any and all of the typical theatrical equipment packages and provide all coordination and responsibility.

Lighting

Today all stage lighting systems operate on a dimmer-per-circuit basis. Each lighting fixture is plugged into a circuit outlet that is wired directly to a dimmer. That dimmer is controlled by the lighting control console. Each fixture can be controlled separately or groups according to the needs of the design. The dimmers are located in a dedicated room; the circuit outlets are arrayed throughout the theater and the control console is located in a control room at the rear of the main floor. A network of control outlets, running Ethernet, allows the console to be operated from a number of locations within

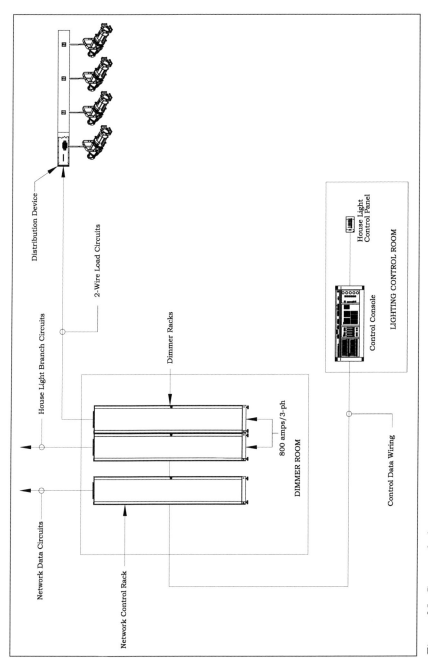

Distribution Device

2-Wire Load Circuits

House Light Branch Circuits

Dimmer Racks

Network Data Circuits

Network Control Rack

800 amps/3-ph

DIMMER ROOM

House Light
Control Panel

Control Console

LIGHTING CONTROL ROOM

Control Data Wiring

Figure 25: Generic lighting system.

the theater. The Ethernet network also allows control of moving lights, color scrollers and other lighting accessories.

The dimmers, dimmer racks, circuit devices, panels, etc. are fabricated by the manufacturer and delivered to the theater for installation by the electrical contractor. The electrical contractor supplies and installs the conduit, wire and wire connections required for the stage lighting system to function.

Although it is the theater consultant who will determine the parameters of the lighting system, it is the electrical engineer who will determine conduit size, conduit fill, wire sizes, terminations, power requirements and satisfaction of both the NEC and local building code. To contain capital and operating costs, the electrical engineer will often apply a *diversity* factor to the power required for the lighting system. Since it is very unlikely that all dimmers will be simultaneously fully loaded and at full intensity, the power requirement can be reduced.

Rigging

The most common rigging system installed in proscenium theaters is a single purchase counterweight rigging system. This permanently installed system allows scenery, lighting, etc. hung on the rigging batten to be counterbalanced on a 1:1 basis. For every 100 pounds placed on the pipe batten, 100 pounds of counterweight is placed on the counterweight arbor. For every foot the pipe moves, the arbor also moves one foot. This system allows easy, safe movement of the batten to execute scenery and lighting cues.

Rigging sets are placed parallel to the proscenium opening and are usually spaced 6", 8", 9" or 12" on center. The density of rigging sets will depend upon the program and the budget. Each rigging set includes: headblock, loftblock, arbor, tension sheave, pipe batten, rope lock and wire rope. Common to all rigging sets in a given installation are: t-bar guide battery, locking rail, counterweight and index strip light.

Double purchase counterweight rigging is similar to single purchase, except that the rigging batten is counterbalanced on a 2:1 basis. For every 100 pounds placed on the batten, 200 pounds is placed on the arbor. For every two feet the pipe moves, the arbor moves one foot. This system is employed when the rigging is operated from a gallery above the stage.

Motorized rigging is a 'dead-haul' system where pipe battens are lifted and supported by motors, gearing and brakes. Small systems are controlled by

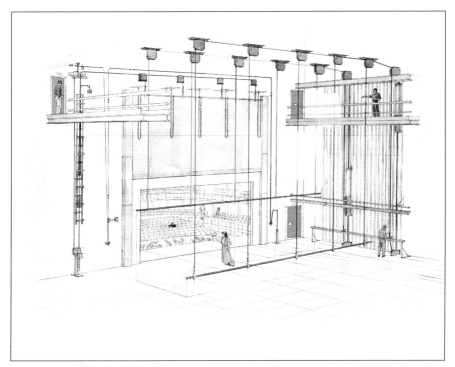

Figure 26: Counterweight rigging system © JR Clancy.

up/down switches. Larger installations may employ a computerized control console that can create presets and cues. A motorized rigging system can be advantageous in a renovation of a proscenium theater that does not have a full fly loft. Whether manual or motorized, the stage rigging is typically designed, fabricated, delivered and installed by the rigging contractor.

Infrastructure must be designed to physically accommodate and to support and sustain the loads imposed by the rigging. Most building types have fixed (i.e. unchanging) loads and do not require access to the structure. Stage rigging imposes ever changing loads upon the building structure and must be accessible. Although there is a fixed upper limit to how much weight can possibly be placed on the rigging, the load will rarely be uniform and will, more likely, create areas with concentrated loads next to others with only minimal loading. Structural engineers address this problem by applying a *diversity* factor. This allows the rigging infrastructure to be designed to accommodate the unique loading conditions encountered in a theater.

Figure 27: Floor mounted seating.

Seating

An audience seating system is designed, fabricated, delivered and installed by the seating manufacturer. Seating for theaters is usually upholstered, with a velour fabric, supported by an iron standard with wood armrests and self-rising seats (which is a code requirement). Seats in a given row will share an armrest with the adjacent seat except for the end seats, which will have an individual end standard. Aisle lighting is often accommodated within the end standard at the end of the seating rows.

Seating mounted to a flat, sloped or shallow stepped row will be floor mounted. Seating on rows with a *row rise* (height difference) of 1 foot or more is usually mounted to the row riser.

Demountable seats, usually in pairs, are installed in the theater to address a number of needs: wheelchair and companion seating, creation of a sound mix position, creation of camera positions (for television broadcast), and on the orchestra lift. When one of these circumstances arises, the seats are removed for the length of time required. In all other respects, the seats are identical to the other seats.

Whether floor or riser mounted, the structure must be designed to accept and support the seating. Most manufacturers recommend 3" of concrete that is free of obstructions (such as rebar and conduit). An orchestra lift may require additional wood blocking or other additional structure to support demountable seating.

Sound

The sound system is comprised of four primary systems. The sound reinforcement system amplifies the words/music onstage and broadcasts it over the loudspeakers to the audience. The intercom system is a two-way communication system for technical staff to use during a performance. The monitor/page system sends an audio feed, of the events on stage, to all the dressing rooms and other backstage support spaces. In addition, it allows those

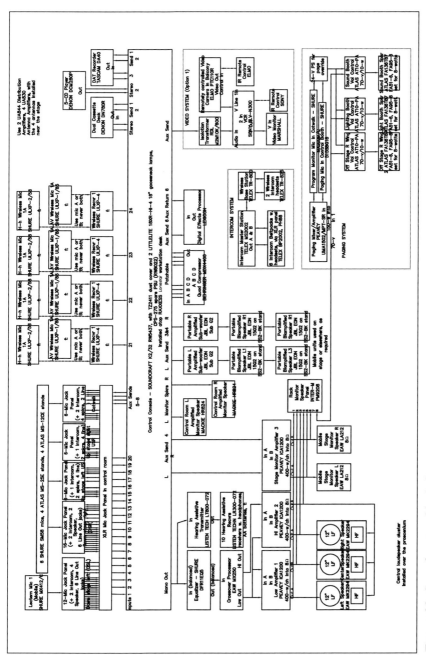

Figure 28: Sound system block diagram.

spaces to be paged from the stage. The assisted listening system provides a wireless audio feed broadcast to headsets worn by audience members (who might have difficulty hearing the performance). The provision of an assisted listening system is mandated by the ADA and incorporated into most building codes.

The sound system includes a network of different circuits distributed throughout the stage and audience seating area. Microphone, line level, intercom, speaker, 70-volt speaker, data and video wires all end up in sound equipment racks located in the sound control room. From there, they are patched into various equipment as required for a production.

The sound system equipment, panels, wire and wire terminations are provided by the sound contractor. The conduit system, however, is designed by the electrical engineer and provided and installed by the electrical contractor. Occasionally this can create a jurisdictional dispute between union (electrical) and non-union (sound) workers. If the sound system is purchased as part of Division 16, this is not an issue.

The signals generated by elements of the sound system are very sensitive

---

ALLOWABLE CONDUIT TYPES:
1. ELECTRIC METALLIC CONDUIT (EMT)
2. GALVANIZED RIGID STEEL CONDUIT (GRS)
3. PVC–COATED RIGID STEEL CONDUIT IN CONCRETE SLAB

NOTE: PVC CONDUIT SHALL NOT BE ALLOWED FOR ANY SOUND & COMMUNICATION SYSTEMS WIRING. NO EXCEPTIONS !

MINIMUM SEPARATION REQUIRED BETWEEN SOUND & COMMUNICATION SYSTEM CONDUIT SIGNAL LEVELS

WIRING SIGNAL LEVEL	MICROPHONE LEVEL GROUP – A & B	SPARE – SOUND SYSTEM GROUP – C	R/F LEVEL GROUP – D	INTERCOM LEVEL & DC CONTROL GROUP – E	SOUND SYSTM LOUDSPEAKER LEVEL GROUP – F	70.7 VOLT LOUDSPEAKER LEVEL GROUP – G	ISOLATED GROUND A–C POWER LEVEL
MICROPHONE LEVEL GROUP – A & B	ADJACENT	ADJACENT	3"	6"	9"	12"	18"
SPARE – SOUND SYSTEM GROUP – C	ADJACENT	ADJACENT	3"	6"	9"	12"	18"
R/F & VIDEO LEVEL GROUP – D	3"	3"	ADJACENT	3"	6"	9"	15"
INTERCOM LEVEL & DC CONTROL GROUP – E	6"	6"	3"	ADJACENT	3"	6"	12"
SOUND SYSTEM LOUDSPEAKER LEVEL GROUP – F	9"	9"	6"	3"	ADJACENT	3"	9"
70.7 VOLT LOUDSPEAKER LEVEL GROUP – G	12"	12"	9"	6"	3"	ADJACENT	6"

Figure 29: Sound system conduit layout.

to outside electrical and magnetic interference. Different wire types are not usually run in the same conduit. Certain conduit spacing between conduits carrying different sound wires (determined by the sound system designer) is documented in the Construction Documents and must be monitored in the field. Failure to observe proper conduit spacing can introduce noise into the system that will be difficult to remove.

Stage Machinery

Typical stage machinery includes: orchestra lifts, turntables, stage lifts, motorized platforms, motorized house curtains and motorized pipe battens. In the United States, most of these specialized systems are found only in large professional theaters or opera houses. Of this equipment, an orchestra lift is to be found most often in theaters.

An orchestra lift is a motorized platform located downstage of the front edge of the stage. The platform has three basic positions: at stage level (where it functions as a stage extension), at audience level (where additional seating may be placed upon it) and below the audience level (for use as an orchestra pit). Orchestra lifts may be driven by different systems: hydraulic (although this is not often specified today), screw-jack and tubular thrust screw (a.k.a slinky). Each of these has its pro's and con's that should be evaluated to determine which is best for a particular installation. Stage machinery is usually supplied and installed by the rigging contractor.

The design load of an orchestra lift can be many tens of thousands of pounds and the structural engineer must design appropriate foundations to support it. In addition, the side walls of the pit must include two

Figure 30: Orchestra lift

slots, which will house the lift guide rails. These rails do not see a significant structural load and are used to prevent the lift from swaying during operation. Last, the power requirements of the lift may differ from the rest of the facility. Dimming systems, sound systems and general power for the theater (in the US) typically employs 120/208 volt service. 227 volt service may be supplied for general purpose fluorescent lighting, but an orchestra lift may require 408 volt service. The electrical engineer, with input from the theater consultant, will determine the electrical service for all theatrical equipment.

Any motorized theatrical device can be dangerous if it is misused or if safety features are not incorporated into the design. The design of an orchestra lift, or any other motorized system should take the following items into consideration:

- The control panel should be key-enabled.
- The control panel should be located so the operator can see the lift moving. This is often accomplished using a pendant (that can plug into the main control panel or into a receptacle on the lift itself.
- An oversized emergency stop button, which instantaneously stops movement of the lift, must be incorporated into the main panel and the pendant.
- Pressure sensitive tape (astragals) should be placed at all shear points (i.e. where the lift passes close to the building structure and an object might get caught).
- Activation of the astragal should stop movement of the lift and move it 2"-3" in the opposite direction. This prevents damage to equipment and to any unfortunate body part.

FFE

Fixtures, Furniture and Equipment include all the loose ends that are required for day-to-day activities. In the theater, FFE can include: brooms, ladders, hardware, chairs, music stands, drapery hampers, file cabinets, booms and bottom pipe, personnel lifts, gels, gobos, template holders, wardrobe racks, washers, dryers, garbage cans, dumpsters, sash cord, hemp, stage manager's box, chorus risers, orchestra risers, orchestra pit filler platforms, tools, dance floor, refrigerator … and the list goes on.

FFE items can be purchased directly and without going through the bid process. For convenience, or if there is no FFE budget, it may be better to purchase certain items as part of the lighting or rigging system. Often these items are purchased, as they are needed, using funds from operating expenses after the facility opens.

8 THE STAGE

The stage is the area where the performance takes place – the area that is visible to the audience. Its size and relation to the audience depends upon the program for the theater. Historically, the relationship between the performer and audience has included a great variety of configurations. Many ad hoc performance spaces take advantage of the unique features of a particular space, but, most theaters built today fall into one of the following forms:

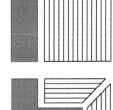

> **Proscenium** where the audience is on one side and the performance takes place behind the proscenium arch.

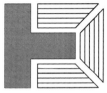

> **Thrust** where the audience is seated on three sides around the stage.

> **Arena** where the audience is seated on all sides of the stage.

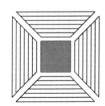

> **Black Box** where the seating/stage arrangement is flexible.

Shape, Size and Construction

The shape and size of the stagehouse will be developed by the theater consultant in conjunction with the users and architect. This is where having done your homework comes into play (see chapter 2). Factors involved in this determination may include:

Figure 31: Theater forms.

> What form will the stage take?

> Is the stage for dedicated use (i.e. a concert hall) or multiple uses (i.e. a road house)?

> Is a symphony orchestra part of the program?

> Is there more than one performance space in the facility?

> Will the stage house touring attractions?

> Is there any large equipment that is to be stored offstage? (i.e. orchestra shell or piano)

Is there any unique activity or equipment that must be accommodated?

The stagehouse itself is usually constructed using steel and concrete block or concrete panels. To prevent stray reflections, the stagehouse walls, including the fly loft, should be painted flat black. If budget is a concern, the black paint can stop ten feet, or so, above the elevation of the hard proscenium opening.

Stage Floor

For most theaters, the stage floor should be a resilient wood construction (to prevent foot injuries to dancers, for example). At the same time, it must be able to sustain the weight of heavy scenery and equipment. A typical arrangement includes neoprene pads, sleepers, plywood sub-floor and a finished floor. A stage floor designed to support 125-150 pounds/square foot is suitable for almost all theaters. If the floor is to be trapped, additional considerations will need to be taken into account by the theater consultant and structural engineer.

The intended use of the theater will determine the specific stage floor detail;

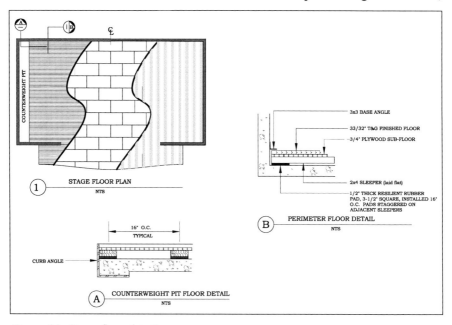

Figure 32: Stage floor details.

especially the type of material used for the finished floor. A dedicated concert or recital hall may employ oak or maple, which are hardwoods, for their appearance. A road house will require a durable, but softer wood, such as edge-grain pine, that will easily accept the occasional nail and stage screw. A university theater, used to train students, that will see the stage floor painted repeatedly and filled with nails and screws (to anchor scenery) may be better served without a finished floor. In this case 4' x 8' Duron®/Masonite panels can provide a surface that will accept paint, nails, screws, minor damage and can easily be replaced when it becomes worn.

Wings

Wings are the off-stage areas immediately to the right and left of the stage and are masked from the audience's view. The wings serve as a staging area for performers awaiting their entrance, scenery awaiting its entrance, prop tables, quick-change rooms, motors and controls for scenery and storage. Some theaters also have a "wing" upstage. This is often found when circulation from the loading area into the stage is via the rear of the stage. It is also found in opera houses where full-stage size wagons move sets on and offstage. Many theaters that have a large orchestra shell (enclosure) will design an upstage niche to house it (instead of using valuable wing space).

In a proscenium theater the wing containing the counterweight rigging is usually smaller than the opposite side. If the persons operating the rigging are too far away, they cannot see the moving scenery or the performers. The width of the wing without rigging should ideally be equal to the distance from the center-line of the stage to the edge of the proscenium opening. Often circulation to a scene shop or to the loading area will be from this side. At a minimum each wing should be the same depth as the stage

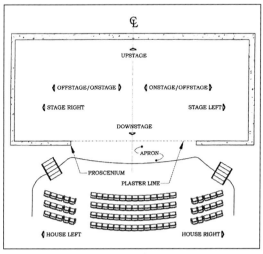

Figure 33: Generic stage diagram.

and wide enough to accommodate the masking draperies and mask the wing from audience view.

Storage

Storage is the one thing a theater can never have enough of. Necessary and unnecessary items accumulate over the life of a theater and there needs to be someplace to put them! Often during value engineering it is the storage areas that are first removed – and it should be the first. After all, would you rather not have a scene shop or costume shop? That having been said, storage is a critical aspect of the day-to-day operation of the theater and one that should not cavalierly be dismissed.

The size, shape and total square footage of storage needed is dependent upon the nature of the theater. Opera houses, in which everything is designed on a grand scale, will need to store 3-dimensional scenery that can be 30-40 feet tall. Often, several sub-basements are provided for the storage of complete opera sets. Full stage elevators move these massive sets to and from storage.

Other items that required dedicated storage are: furniture, props, costumes, stair units, platforms, platform legs, flats, door and window units, draperies, rigging supplies, lighting fixtures, sound system equipment, musical instruments, pianos, musicians' chairs, music stands and all the disposable supplies and accessories needed for the theatrical systems.

Ideally, storage areas should be located adjacent to the area/activity they serve. Instrument storage can be on the level below the stage and near the orchestra pit. Music stands and chairs can also be located in this area. Scenery storage may be located in an area between a stage wing and the scene shop. Costume storage, laundry and costume shop should be adjacent and have easy access to the dressing rooms. If, for some reason, a storage area must be located away from its related activity then proper circulation, such as a freight elevator, should be considered.

Technical Circulation

Performers and stage hands require clear and direct horizontal pathways between the stage and support spaces. They also require vertical pathways: from second floor dressing rooms to the stage and from the stage to the fly floor, grid and lighting catwalks. The stage and wing area should have access to its four corners from a surrounding corridor. Vertical circulation (stairs and elevators) should also be located off this corridor (at the four corners of the stage).

Loading doors (at the stage and scene shop) and freight elevators should be provided for horizontal and vertical circulation of equipment, sets, lighting, costumes, etc within the building.

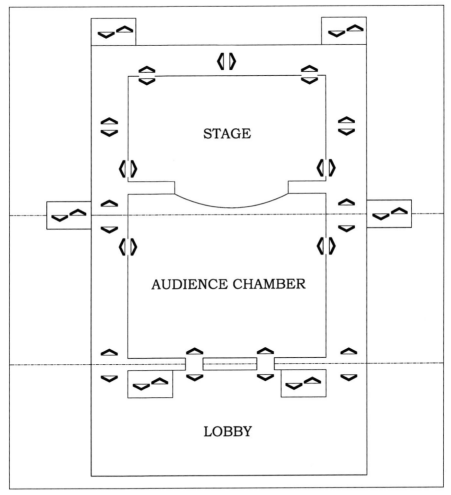

Figure 34: Circulation diagram.

9 BACKSTAGE

Backstage can refer to the wings or any area outside of the audience's view; but when considering the design and layout of a theater, it is taken to mean the various spaces necessary to support the production. The support spaces, common to most theaters, are briefly described in this section.

The efforts of the architect and design team inevitably focus on the lobby and audience chamber. This is not a bad thing as these are significant aspects of the theater. What should be remembered are the people who will work in the theater 24 hours a day/7 days a week/365 days a year. The stage and backstage areas must be designed with the needs of these folks firmly in mind. The backstage area is comprised of various work rooms each with very specific needs. Room dimensions, ceiling heights, ventilation, plumbing and electrical needs must be specifically addressed as well as circulation between them and between them and the stage.

Staff of the theater will, of course, become familiar with the backstage layout and circulation paths. Outside groups, such as traveling shows loading into a road house, will need to have backstage areas arranged in a sensible manner so that performers and crew, who will only be in your theater for a few days, can get around. For these venues, well-designed signage is especially important.

Backstage is where you will find performers, stage crew, production staff, musicians: in short all the people responsible for creating the "magic" onstage. They deserve a comfortable, well-planned and thought-out work environment that will not hinder but help them in their day-to-day activities.

Dressing Rooms

The dressing room is where a performer changes out of their street clothes and into their costumes. The performer may return to the dressing room during intermission and may entertain guests after the performance. It is also where they put on/take off make-up, shower and return to their street clothes. Dressing rooms may also be provided for musicians and stage-hands.

Depending upon the size and program of a theater, a variety of different size dressing rooms are included. Regardless of its size, each dressing room

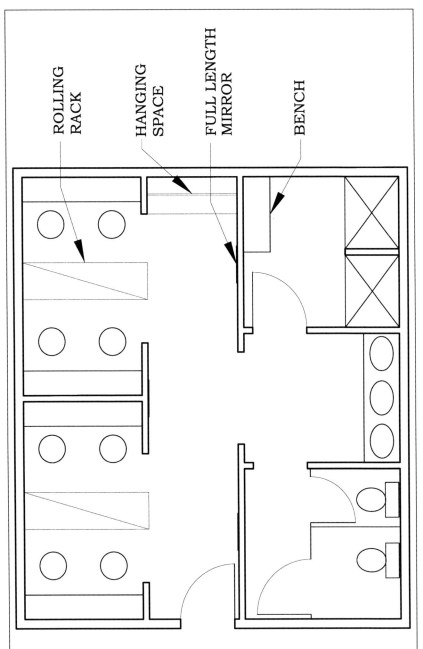

ROLLING RACK

HANGING SPACE

FULL LENGTH MIRROR

BENCH

Figure 35: Chorus dressing room.

will include: make-up stations, chairs, toilet and shower, hanging space for street clothes and costumes and a full-length mirror. Historically, space for dressing rooms was not a priority for the producers who built them. They were usually small, cramped and stacked vertically on either side of the stage, accessible only by narrow stairs. The show's star and principal players were assigned the lower floors and the chorus to the topmost. Theaters designed today include much more spacious accommodations for performers, but the hierarchy remains.

A star dressing room is often a small suite for a visiting artist or other prestigious person. It may include a sitting area, television and kitchenette. When not in use by a VIP, it may be used by two performers. In some cases it is known as a double. This room will be located very near to the stage.

A quad dressing room is sized for four performers and may or may not include a sitting area. In a musical comedy, with a large cast, the quad dressing rooms will be occupied by principals and supporting players. After the star dressing room, the quads are closest to the stage.

A chorus dressing room takes its name from the chorus members who use it. This dressing room typically accommodates eight performers, but may be sized for up to sixteen. The chorus dressing rooms are, traditionally, the farthest from the stage and the ones that may be on a second or third floor above the stage.

Musician's dressing rooms or changing rooms are similar to chorus rooms (designed to accommodate a large group of people). Two changing rooms, with a common lounge area, are desirable for male and female musicians. A similar arrangement is also made for the stage-hands.

Rehearsal Rooms

Historically theaters were not built with any rehearsal rooms. In fact, the theater was not even booked until the scenery and lighting were ready for installation. Rehearsals took place in rented spaces until technical and dress rehearsals occurred. Today, this remains the case for most Broadway theaters in New York City. New theaters, with sufficient space and budget, will include one or more rehearsal rooms within the facility. These can be used by resident organizations or rented.

A rehearsal room should be a double height room that is, ideally, the same dimensions as the stage plus an additional 25% for circulation. (Secondary rehearsal rooms can be smaller). Mirrors should be placed along one wall with

Figure 36: McGuire Pavillion dance studio.

curtains to cover them. The floor should be a resilient wood construction to prevent foot injuries to dancers and other performers. Permanent or portable dance barres are desirable as well as windows to allow natural light.

College and university rehearsal rooms often double as performance spaces. In this case a pipe grid may be installed along with a minimal lighting and rigging system.

Scene Shop

Broadway theaters and many professional theater companies have scenery for their productions built by an outside scene shop and delivered to the theater. College, university and other educational theater facilities most often fabricate their own scenery as part of the curriculum.

The scene shop should be a double height room with direct access to the loading dock and to the stage. There must be sufficient space for fixed power tools, work tables and a clear area for trial assembly of larger scenic units. It must also have space for lumber, metals and other set building materials, as well as hand tools and hardware. Room lighting should provide levels of illumination commensurate with the operation of power tools and of small scale, detailed work.

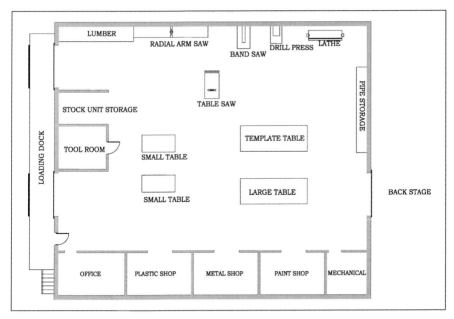

Figure 37: Generic scene shop.

Paint Shop

The paint shop is used to paint large scenic units and drops. Ideally, it is located adjacent to both the scene shop and the stage to facilitate the flow of scenery. It should be large enough to accommodate one or both of the methods used to paint a large drop. A *paint frame* is a motorized, vertical frame that can be raised and lowered (using a slot in the floor) to allow different sections to be painted, while the painter stands on the floor. The other painting method is to lay the drop flat on the floor. Using this method, the painter may walk on the drop and/or use extension rods to reach areas of the drop from its perimeter. Circulation space around the drop is required and the floor should be a resilient construction with a finished floor surface that will accept nails.

The paint shop will require lockable storage for paints, brushes and other accessories. Stock flats are also often stored here and racks for them should be incorporated as "built-ins". Most scene paints are made from latex or other non-toxic materials. It can be expected, however, that the scenic design will require the use of toxic materials. A dedicated exhaust system, venting noxious fumes to the outside, will address this issue.

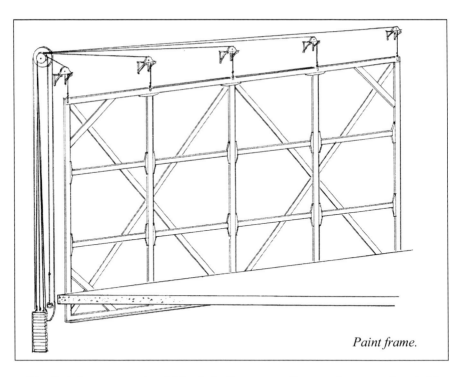

Paint frame.

The lighting system should include fluorescent fixtures for general activities and incandescent fixtures to allow the scene designer and scene painter an impression of how the drop will look under the stage lights. Each should be controlled separately and provide a high level of illumination. Natural light, via clerestory windows, is also desirable.

Costume Shop

The costume shop, for a college or university theater, should also be a double height room located near to a laundry room, costume storage area and the dressing rooms. Natural light is desirable coupled with full-spectrum room lighting. A viewing area lit with incandescent fixtures will allow the costume designer an impression of how costume will look onstage. The detailed nature of sewing and costume construction requires much higher illumination levels than a typical classroom. Lighting illumination levels, for different tasks, can be found in the IES Lighting Handbook.

The costume shop must be sized to accommodate 4'x6' cutting tables, sewing

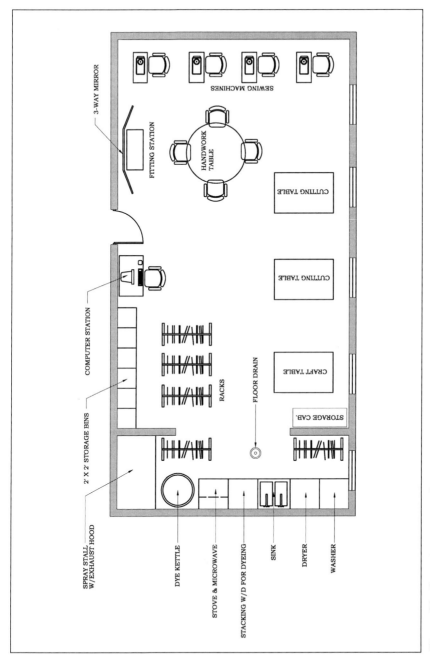

Figure 38: Generic costume shop.

machines, steam irons, fitting areas and built-ins for storage of fabrics, thread, buttons, and other materials. The room will also need space for rolling racks and dress mannequins. An adjacent area, with a large sink is required for dying of materials, as well as a vented spray booth.

Costume storage is critical for facilities that fabricate their own costumes and sometimes recycle them for different productions. The storage room should be climate controlled, well lit, and allow easy access to the costumes. Common storage solutions include permanent pipe racks along the walls and/or suspended from the ceiling and tiered hanging space.

Wardrobe Shop
A wardrobe shop is similar to a costume shop only smaller in scale as it is not intended to be used to construct costumes, but solely to maintain them.

Properties Shop
Properties or props include furniture and other items handled by the actors during a performance. Their fabrication is generally more detailed and requires smaller and more delicate, specialized tools. The prop shop is usually adjacent to the scene shop. Value engineering may move it into the scene shop and sometimes eliminate it altogether. This extreme should be avoided, as the use of props is an integral part of theatrical productions. As with the other spaces discussed, where detail work will be performed, appropriate levels of illumination must be provided.

Lighting/Sound Shop
If possible, separate rooms for maintenance and repair of the stage lighting fixtures and sound equipment should be provided. Each room should have a work bench, tool storage, desk and shelving for equipment awaiting repair. These two rooms may be combined but not at the price of reduced overall space. Fluorescent general lighting with supplemental task lighting, above work surfaces, is acceptable.

Technical Offices
The designers, department heads and staff of a theater will require office space to perform their duties. Each office should be large enough to contain a desk, chair, work table, shelving and guest seating. As with any office, there should

be outlets for power, telephone and Ethernet. Ideally a given office should be near or adjacent to the work area of the person using it (i.e. the costume office should be near the costume shop; the technical director's office should be near the scene shop, etc).

In an educational facility the function of these rooms may be taken by faculty and staff offices and need not be duplicated.

Green Room

There are many speculations on the origins for the name of this room. Spence Porter (from New York University) suggests that a contextual use of the term in 1701, by the English owner-actor/playwright Colley Cibber 1671-1735, indicates he expected people to recognize the term, so it was probably in common use by the end of the 1690s.

Most lexicographers have concluded the term did originate from the color early greenrooms were painted, but no one has any firm reasons as to why they would have been painted green. Whatever its true genesis, a green room is a lounge for performers and crew, where they can relax and receive visitors. It is furnished with tables, couches, comfortable chairs and can include a refrigerator and kitchenette. In educational theaters is also used for meetings, as an ad hoc classroom and all-purpose hang-out for the denizens of the theater.

Dimmer Room

A temperature and humidity controlled space, the dimmer room will house all of the stage lighting dimmer racks for the theater, or theaters (although this is not a hard and fast rule). The room should be located with an eye toward the enormous number of conduits that will converge there and to minimize the distance between the dimmer racks and the majority of the stage lighting circuits. The dimmer room will require a higher than normal ceiling (again, to accommodate the conduit that will enter the room and be fed into the dimmer racks).

Figure 39: Dimmer racks.

Amplifier Room

The requirements of the amplifier room are similar to the dimmer room, except that in lieu of dimmer racks it will contain amplifier racks and other sound equipment racks. Because sound system wiring is sensitive to interference, it should not be located adjacent to the dimmer room.

Orchestra Pit

Musicians, for a performance, will be located in the orchestra pit. Located between the front of the stage and the first row of seats, the orchestra pit allows the musicians to be hidden from view while the conductor remains visible to the performers.

Attendant upon the design of an orchestra pit is circulation to backstage support areas that meets ADA criteria.

Figure 40: Orchestra pit.

Loading Area

Ease of access is a critical factor in the design of the backstage areas and the loading dock is the principal point of entry. Everyone and everything will enter the theater through the loading area. The loading area should provide easy access for trucks and be situated to provide easy and direct access to the stage and backstage areas. This is not only a 'work environment' issue but an operational issue. A well designed loading area will require fewer people and less time to move shows in and out of the theater. Less people + less time = less cost. This is especially so for a road house where absolutely everything must be brought into the theater and then loaded out.

The theater loading dock is the principal access point for all equipment and materials and should be dedicated exclusively for use by the theater. If the dock is shared, then selected loading bays should be dedicated for use by the theater. The number of loading bays will depend on the size and scope of the theater but certain features should always be included.

- The loading dock should be on the same level as the stage.
- The loading dock should be on the same level as the stage.
- The loading dock should be on the same level as the stage.

- Did I mention that the loading dock should be on the same level as the stage?
- Two bays, minimum (in case a vehicle remains overnight).
- The grade in front of the dock must be level (so that heavy things on wheels do not come flying out of the truck).
- Include a dock leveler to allow a smooth transition between the truck and the dock.
- Allow sufficient room for a semi-trailer to maneuver when approaching/leaving the dock.
- Allow a parking area for a semi-trailer (to keep the loading bay available).
- The dock should be covered, heated (in the colder climes) and well-lit

In many older theaters, the loading dock door opens directly onto the stage. A receiving area, between the dock and other spaces in the building, is advantageous as a staging area for load-ins, load-outs and temporary storage. Circulation from this area to dressing rooms and wardrobe room, in addition to the stage, should also be considered.

Stage Door
The stage door is the entry for performers, stagehands, staff and visitors. Ideally it will be adjacent to and have a view of the loading dock to maintain security in both areas. If direct view of the dock is not possible, video

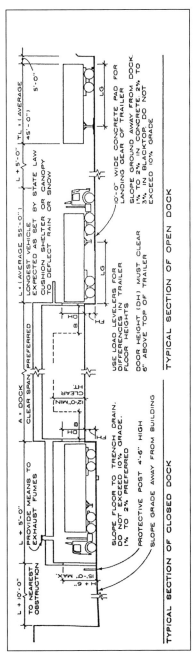

Figure 41: Loading dock diagram.

surveillance may be employed. The stage door often contains a call board and is a meeting place for cast, crew and visitors. If possible this should be designed with a security office and a waiting area with seating.

10 AUDITORIUM

The auditorium is the area where the audience sits. Seating may all be on one level or distributed on multiple levels (balconies). Seating may also located in boxes on the side walls on the main floor and balcony levels. In historic theaters and opera houses, one often finds balcony boxes wrapped around the side wall right up to the proscenium arch.

Figure 42: Hammerstein Theater.

While not especially desirable for seeing the performance, they are very desirable for being "seen" at the performance.

How Many Seats?

As Joe Golden points out in Olympus on Main Street, every seat more, or every seat less, has an impact on something: costs, revenues, sight lines, acoustics, safety and maintenance.

Economically a house should be as large as possible, consistent with the size of the potential audience. Aesthetically it should be no larger than is absolutely necessary for maximum impact of the performance (on the audience). Often the two considerations are in conflict. Sometimes, the size of a house could be increased substantially on the basis of market potential. But, if it gets too big, the aesthetic experience may be so diminished that the market potential drops. Invariably, house size becomes a compromise among the various aesthetic, acoustic, marketing and economic considerations.[1]

Seating and Sightlines

Audience seating and sightline considerations are basic concepts in the design of a theater. The ability of each audience member to see the stage must be

Figure 43: No sightlines, Every-other-row sightlines, Every-row sightlines.

maintained on both vertical and horizontal planes. In addition to good sightlines, the seating arrangement should foster a visually intimate relationship to heighten the emotional connection between performers and audience.

Staggering the seats from row-to-row provides every-other-row sightlines. An audience member will be able to see between the heads of the persons in the row directly in front and over the head of the person seated two rows in front.

Increasing the row rise (the height difference from one row to the next) provides every-row sightlines. An audience member will be able to see over the head of the person directly in front of them.

Seating Arrangements

Fifteen sq. ft/person is a rule of thumb that will provide a preliminary estimate of the auditorium size. The figure includes the seat itself as well as aisle space. Within this area the seats will be arranged to provide the best possible sightlines and intimacy with the stage. There are two seating arrangements commonly used: American and Continental. Each has its pros and cons, as well as its own unique building code requirements. Most theaters use one or the other exclusively. This is not to say, however, that the two cannot be mixed. For a variety of reasons, a theater may employ Amercian style seating on the main floor and Continental in the balconies.

American Seating provides more aisles within the seating area. Although code allows certain exceptions, the general rules are that a seating section with an aisle at each side may contain up to 14 seats. A seating section with an aisle on one side may only contain up to 7 seats. Another way you may find this expressed is that a person need only cross (6) seats to reach an aisle.

The advantage of this arrangement is easy access to all seats and fewer audience exits (compared to Continental seating.) The disadvantage is that aisles will be located where seating could have been. Row to row spacing,

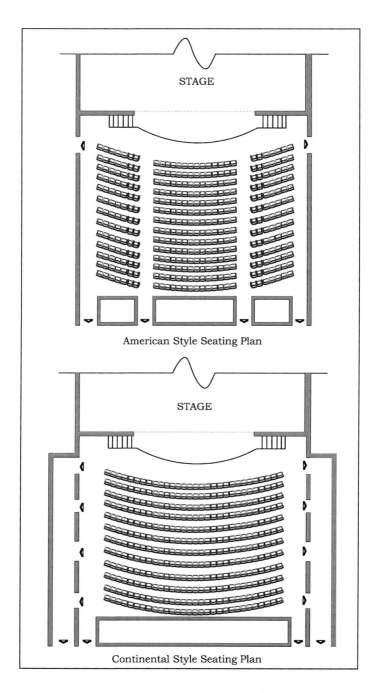

American Style Seating Plan

Continental Style Seating Plan

in theaters built today, will range between 34" and 36". Older theaters may have tighter row to row spacing of as little as 32". While a tight row to row spacing brings more people closer to the stage and creates a more intimate environment, it does not leave much leg room.

Continental seating has uninterrupted seating across a row with aisles located on the extreme sides of the seating area. Thus, all of the available seating "real estate" is populated with seats. Building code requires a row to row spacing of at least 42" so there is plenty of leg room for even the leg-iest patron. The disadvantage is that rows can span as many as 60 seats. A person sitting in the middle of the row will have to cross 30 seats to reach an aisle. If you think about this in reverse, a late-comer will interrupt more people as they move to their seats. Code also requires more exit doors, prescribed spacing of those exits and prescribed egress paths.

The Individual Seat

Theater seating comes in a variety of styles, designs and prices. You can pay as little as $200 for a basic chair or as much as $1,000+ for a custom chair. Whatever your budget: the primary concern should be for audience comfort. The audience should be able to concentrate on the performance and not how sore their bottoms or legs are. Seat selection criteria should include:

- Seat width between 21" and 24", measured from center armrest to center armrest. Older theaters may have seats as narrow as 19" and, as the American media has pointed out, we have gotten too fat for that seat.
- A strong seat back, angled appropriately. The seat back on the main floor will be more gently angled than a balcony seat.
- Sufficient seat padding and contoured seat pans (to prevent sore thighs.)
- A quiet seat-rising mechanism. Code requires that seats be designed so that the seat pan automatically rises when you get up to allow space for egress. It is bad enough when someone must answer the 'call of nature' at an intense, dramatic part of the performance, without having to have the mood broken by the 'squeek' or 'sproing' of a chair.

Public Circulation

Audience circulation is strictly defined by building codes designed to protect the audience. Codes achieve this by specifying: row lengths, row-to-row spacing, aisle widths, aisle locations, door sizes, door locations, door quantities and travel distances (from a given seat to an exit). The seating layout must follow all of the code criteria.

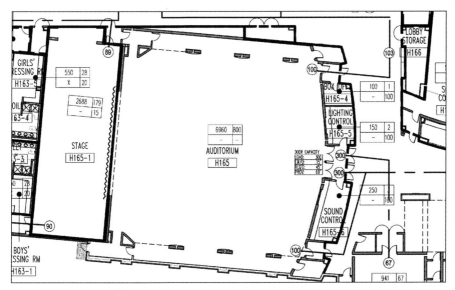

Figure 44: Egress plan.

ADA

The Americans with Disabilities Act Accessibility Guidelines (ADAAG) provide specific standards and details for implementation of the Americans with Disabilities Act. These guidelines are intended for use during the design of a building and many ADAAG criteria have been incorporated into city, state and national building codes.

Of particular concern to us are the following criteria, summarized from Pocket Guide to the ADA, Americans with Disabilities Act Guidelines for Buildings and Facilities, 1997. Edited by Evan Terry Associates, P.C.

- Assisted listening systems are required for all places of public assembly.
- Wheelchair locations, with companion seats, are required for all places of public assembly seating more. (Tables within the ADAAG describe the additional wheelchair locations required as the seat count increases.)
- Wheelchair locations must be distributed among all seating areas, unless the seat count is less than 300.
- Wheelchair circulation from the auditorium onto the stage must be provided.
- Circulation paths for persons with disabilities cannot be segregated from those for able-bodied persons.

TABLE 1108.2.2.1	
ACCESSIBLE WHEEL CHAIR SPACES	
CAPACITY OF SEATING IN ASSEMBLY AREAS	MINIMUM REQUIRED NUMBER OF WHEELCHAIR SPACES
4 to 25	1
26 to 50	2
51 to 100	4
101 to 300	5
301 to 500	6
501 to 5,000	6, plus 1 for each 150 or fraction thereof, between 501 through 5,000
5,000 and over	36 plus 1 for each 200, or fraction thereof, over 5,000

Figure 45: ADA wheelchair.

- All areas of the theater (lobby, auditorium, stage and backstage) must be accessible to persons with disabilities. (While it is not expected that a person in a wheelchair will be working on the gridiron or lighting catwalk, it is expected that they may operate the lighting or sound systems.)

TABLE 1108.2.7.1 RECEIVERS FOR ASSISTIVE LISTENING SYSTEMS		
CAPACITY OF SEATING IN ASSEMBLY AREAS	MINIMUM REQUIRED NUMBER OF RECEIVERS	MINIMUM NUMBER OF RECEIVERS TO BE HEARING-AID COMPATIBLE
50 or less	2	2
51 to 200	2, plus 1 per 25 seats over 50 seats	2
201 to 500	2, plus 1 per 25 seats over 50 seats	1 per 4 receivers
501 to 1,000	20, plus 1 per 33 seats over 500 seats	1 per 4 receivers
1,001 to 2,000	35, plus 1 per 50 seats over 1,000 seats	1 per 4 receivers
Over 2,000	55, plus 1 per 100 seats over 2,000 seats	1 per 4 receivers

Figure 46: Assisted Listening system requirements of the 2003 International Building Code.

Sound and Light Locks

A sound and light lock (SLL) is a vestibule, at each entrance to the auditorium or stage, designed to keep out unwanted noise and light (should someone enter or leave during a performance). The SLL should be compact in design so that when exiting the theater one opens the interior door, takes one step into the SLL, opens the exterior door and exits. Large, irregular shaped SLLs can cause a person to become disoriented in an emergency situation.

The path through a SLL should be a straight line. If this is not possible, a single turn is acceptable but any additional turns should be avoided. Operation of the doors should be silent. If any panic hardware is required, it should be located on the exterior door.

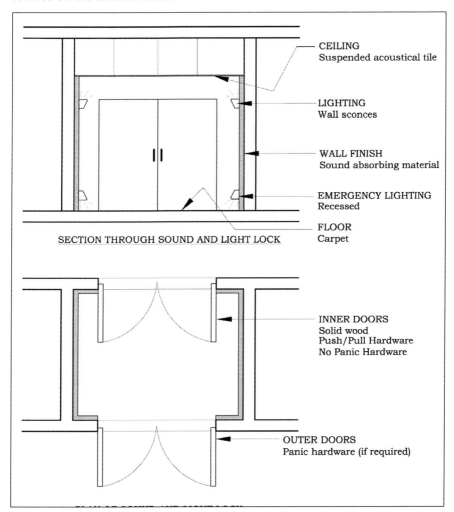

CEILING
Suspended acoustical tile

LIGHTING
Wall sconces

WALL FINISH
Sound absorbing material

EMERGENCY LIGHTING
Recessed

FLOOR
Carpet

SECTION THROUGH SOUND AND LIGHT LOCK

INNER DOORS
Solid wood
Push/Pull Hardware
No Panic Hardware

OUTER DOORS
Panic hardware (if required)

Figure 47: Sound and light lock.

General lighting in a SLL is usually controlled as part of the house lighting system. Code mandated lighting levels (0.2 FC) can be maintained with dedicated lighting recessed into the side walls. These lights should be connected to and powered by the emergency lighting system.

Control Booths

At a minimum dedicated rooms should be provided for: lighting control, sound control, projection and followspots. The lighting and sound control rooms are typically located on the main floor at the rear of the seating area.

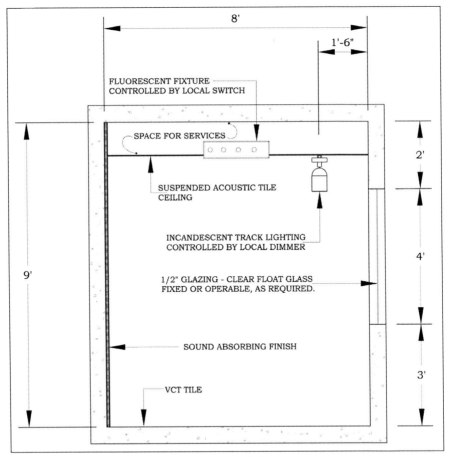

Figure 47a: Typical control booth section model.

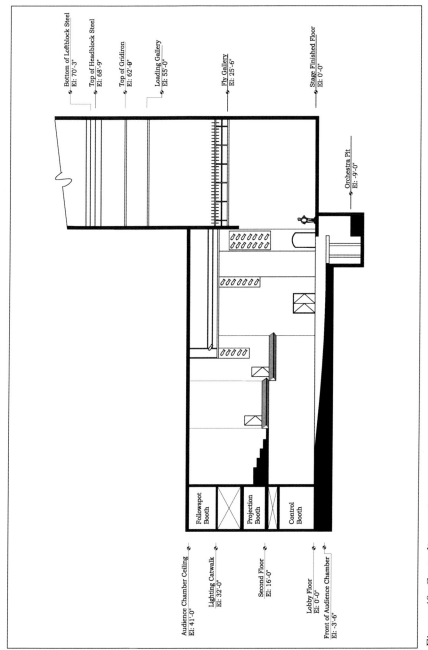

Bottom of Loftblock Steel
El: 70'-3"

Top of Headblock Steel
El: 68'-9"

Top of Gridiron
El: 62'-9"

Loading Gallery
El: 55'-0"

Fly Gallery
El: 25'-6"

Stage Finished Floor
El: 0'-0"

Orchestra Pit
El: -9'-0"

Followspot
Booth

Projection
Booth

Control
Booth

Audience Chamber Ceiling
El: 41'-0"

Lighting Catwalk
El: 32'-0"

Second Floor
El: 16'-0"

Lobby Floor
El: 0'-0"

Front of Audience Chamber
El: -3'-6"

Figure 48: Centreline section.

The projection room is located, ideally, at the rear of the first balcony. The followspot room's location will be dictated by the required angle to the stage.

Each room should be enclosed and have local HVAC and lighting control. Each room should also have a window (aka glazing) to allow a clear and unobstructed view of the stage. Glazing for the projection and followspot booths is usually fixed. Glazing for the sound booth should be operable (so the operator can hear whether the sound cue has come through the speakers). Operable glazing for the lighting control booth is optional.

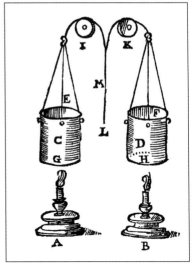

Fig 48a Rennaisance candle.

Stage Lighting Positions

Successful lighting design in the age of gas lighting was primarily measured by whether the audience could see the action on stage. Minimal dimming was possible, but lighting design was not considered a design element of the production. The advent of electric stage lighting dramatically changed both the nature and execution of stage lighting. Stage lighting fixtures with directional beams of light that could be colored and dimmed

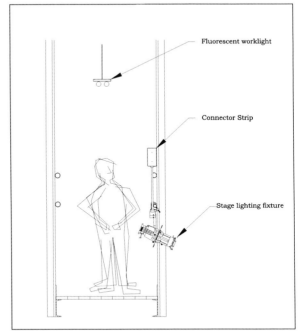

Figure 49: Lighting catwalk.

gave the director and set designer (there weren't any lighting designers in the early 1900s) tremendous options to enhance the appearance and emotional intensity of the show.

Lighting positions over the stage were pretty easy to accommodate, but the only positions available in the house were the balcony rail (with a very flat angle) and the side balcony boxes. In both cases, the lighting was exposed. These positions are still used today along with a ceiling cove position (providing a more flattering lighting angle.) Depending upon the interior design, other lighting positions are often included in the auditorium. These lighting positions may be masked from audience view or not. Whatever architectural form these positions take, they should accommodate an appropriate number of lights and be easily accessible.

House Lighting

The house lighting is sometimes designed by an architectural lighting designer, but most often by the electrical engineer. It is mentioned here as a reminder that the house light fixtures must be accessible for re-lamping. Keep an eye on this; you'd be surprised at how often it slips through the cracks.

Acoustic Concerns

Acoustics are the qualities of the room that affect the sound you hear. The quality of the sound that reaches the audience from the stage is a combination of direct sound from the stage and sound reflected from the surfaces in the hall. The object is to balance these two kinds of sound so that everyone may hear the performance clearly; without any distortion and as the performers intend. Adding to the complexity is that a dramatic play; an opera, a symphony concert, an amplified musical, etc, each have their own optimum balance, which, of course, is significantly different from the others.

Acoustics must also be considered for the performers: in terms of how they hear themselves as well as how they hear the audience response to the performance. Architectural features that impact room acoustics include:

- The overall three dimensional shape of the room
- The volume of the room (height, width and length)
- Balconies (size, configuration, overhang, railing)
- Seat count, areas and distribution
- Seat materials
- Articulation of room surfaces

- Room materials and finishes and their locations
- Whether room finishes are reflective (hard) or absorptive (soft)

Acoustics are perhaps the most controversial aspect of theater design because it is so little understood by other members of the design team, and because many of the acoustician's recommendations may appear counter-intuitive. This is why it is imperative, as we discussed in chapter 3, that an acoustician be included as part of your design team.

The sound you hear is but one part of the acoustician's domain. The other part is the sound you don't hear. Noise and vibration control is the work performed by the acoustician to limit unwanted noise from the stage and audience. Working closely with the architect and engineers, the acoustician ensures that the theater is designed for absolute quiet. Awareness and attention to these issues is paramount to eliminate unwanted sound (i.e. noise) from the theater.

Some noise and vibration issues are:
- Location of mechanical equipment
- Routing of ducts, pipe and conduit
- Duct, pipe and conduit mounting details
- Buffer zones between quiet and noisy spaces
- Structural isolation between quiet and noisy spaces (to prevent vibration bourn noise)
- Equipment mounting details (to prevent vibration bourn noise)
- Wall penetration details

If these issues are not addressed during design and monitored during construction, the theater may be saddled with noise for its entire life. Sometimes it is worth spending money on this type of problem, if you get good advice from a qualified consultant. An acoustics consultant should be able to help assess the costs and benefits of addressing these problems. The best and least expensive way to reduce noise is to keep noisy spaces (i.e. mechanical equipment rooms) and quiet spaces as far apart as possible.

---

[1] Catherine Brown, et. al Building for the Arts, 1984, 1989. Western States Arts Federation. p.114

11 LOBBY

The lobby is the area where the audience assembles before entering the theater proper. Aside from the practical services it provides, the lobby represents the first phase of the theatergoing experience. It is the buffer between the real world and the magical world of the theater, and where you can meet friends and share the anticipation of the performance to come. Its design should help set the audience's expectations for the performance. As the warm-up act is to the main attraction, the lobby is to the theatrical performance. It is an integral part of the facility.

Many older theaters have lobbies that are small, cramped or non-existent. Today, budget permitting, the lobby is a more expansive, large scale space. Today's economics of operation require that all areas of the theater be put to use to generate income, so the lobby may also be used for fundraising events,

Figure 50: Metropolitan Opera lobby.

meetings, art exhibitions, weddings, performances, fashion shows and any other event that can be attracted.

How Big is the Lobby?
Many theaters built in the late 19th century/early 20th century had small to non-existent lobbies: New York City's Broadway theaters are an example of this style. Some 21st century performing arts centers have huge, spacious lobbies that span several levels and serve as gathering spaces for a variety of non-theater events and performances. Other theaters fall somewhere in between.

For planning purposes, 9 sq. ft. per person is a good starting place. This number includes: restrooms, box office, concessions, bar and general circulation. That number may grow to 15 sq. ft. per person, or shrink to 3 sq. ft. per person depending upon a number of factors, such as:

- Site conditions (there may just not be enough room for a spacious lobby)
- Geographic location (a theater in Florida may reduce indoor lobby space in exchange for an outdoor plaza, while a theater in South Dakota, with cold winters, will definitely require indoor lobby for every patron.)
- Budget, budget, budget.

House Manager's Office
The house manager is responsible for the safety and comfort of the audience, and the relevant office should be immediately adjacent to the lobby. As with any administrative office, it should be large enough for the house manager and staff.

First Aid Room/Stations
The first aid room should be located adjacent to the lobby and easily accessible to emergency personnel. The room should include a bed, toilet and first aid supplies. Theaters with balconies and multi-venue facilities should make provision for first aid stations to be located in each venue's lobby and on the balcony levels.

A benefit of the ADA is an increased awareness of the potential medical condition of the audience. Band-aids, Mercurochrome and ice-packs are no longer sufficient. Facilities are expected to have defribulators, wheelchairs, oxygen and personnel who know how to use them and provide first aid (including CPR).

Ushers

Theaters with full-time ushers often include specific male and female locker rooms with a common area where they can change from their street clothes and where schedules and other notices may be posted. This room does not need to be close to the lobby but is generally located on the FOH side of the building. Theaters with volunteer ushers expect them to arrive dressed for work and do not usually provide a changing area.

Concessions

Concessions include food, drink and souvenir items. These areas may be permanent, portable or a combination of the two. They should be distributed in multiple locations on each lobby level to service the high volume occurring during intermissions. Some theaters include a gift shop connected to the lobby that is open during non-performance times. Traveling shows often have their own portable kiosk where they sell CDs, posters, souvenir programs, caps, etc.

Catering

To satisfy the non-performance uses of the lobby, many new theaters include a catering kitchen. This is not a full-scale restaurant kitchen but one that is designed to provide a caterer room to prep, warm-up and serve. Non-public circulation should be provided as well as a separate loading area.

Food and Beverage

Food and beverage service can run the gamut from peanuts, candy, and soda to gourmet aprés-theater, sit-down dinners with vintage wines. Some facilities include restaurant spaces operated by the facility or by an outside vendor that may be open during non-performance times. An up-scale dining experience can be a significant part of the theater-going experience. On the down-side, the nature of the restaurant business can be economically dicey. To whatever degree these options are pursued, non-public circulation should be provided as well as a separate loading area.

His and Hers

We have all witnessed the seemingly inevitable lines winding out of the ladies room during intermission. At a 2004 performance of *Fiddler on the Roof*, at the Marquis Theater in New York, there were lines out of the men's room, as well, that had not diminished even when the audience recall lights blinked. Not only did some audience members miss the beginning of the second act, but the performers and those already seated had to endure the distraction of late-comers finding their way in the dark.

Building codes presume that the audience will be half men and half women and prescribe that one place be provided for every so many women and one place for every so many men. Depending upon the seat-count, these minimum requirements may or may not be sufficient. Sometimes restroom minimums are observed to contain costs. This is a short-sighted measure that will impact the theater for its entire life and can also impact the financial bottom-line. To insure a satisfied audience, that will want to return, the following guidelines should be observed.

- Assume that 70% of every audience will be women
- Distribute restrooms on all lobby levels
- Locate men's and women's restrooms on all levels (don't alternate)
- Restrooms should be easy to find
- Avoid architectural "pinch" points at the entrances
- Provide a lounge area in the men's room too (for dads with young children)

Coat Check

Coat check rooms should be located to one side of the lobby to accommodate the crush at the end of the show (without blocking traffic out of the theater). The rules of thumb are that (12) coats can be hung for every foot of hanger space and, there should be hanger space for 50% of the seating capacity. Often, the coat check also serves as the distribution point for assisted listening headsets. If this is the case, storage space for headsets, batteries and chargers must be included as well as extra counter space.

Entry Vestibule

The entry vestibule is a weather vestibule between the outside and the lobby. It does not have to be large, although it can be; it sometimes acts as a pre-lobby, circulating people to different theaters within a performing arts center. The vestibule works to keep the lobby warm or cool and, in common with the SLLs, it helps to block outside noise from entering the building.

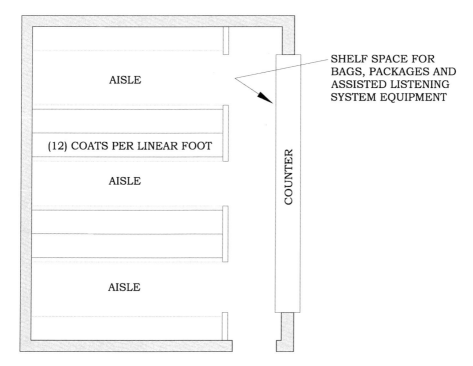

Figure 51: Coat room.

Public Circulation

Circulation in the lobby should guide people to and from those areas they are likely to go: box office, restrooms, concessions, elevators and the auditorium. The intermission will see the greatest activity in the lobby and its design should direct and move the flow of people within the time allotted. Theaters with more than one lobby level should have all audience amenities present on each level.

Box Office

The box office is actually a small suite of offices with different functions. The "front" office sells tickets to the public. The number of ticket window, or wickets, will depend on the size of the facility, but will have a minimum of three: current sales, future sales and will-call (where previously purchased tickets may be picked up immediately prior to a performance). The "back"

Figure 52: NY State Theater box office.

office consists of general work space, secure areas for handling and storing cash, storage for equipment and supplies, computer server, conference room and manager's office.

Professional theaters require access to the ticket windows during performance and non-performance times. A location adjacent to the entry vestibule allows non-performance use without opening the theater lobby, but can create a bottleneck before a show. Older theaters, and some new ones too, have ticket windows in the lobby. As with the coat check, the ticket windows should be to one side of the lobby so as not to impede the flow of persons who already have their tickets. Some theaters maintain a single window facing the street for non-performance times when there is not much traffic.

It is important to remember that, although the primary function of the box office is to sell tickets, it is also a prominent "face" that creates the audience's impression of the facility.

Although ticket sales are now made with credit cards, by telephone and online, there is still a portion purchased with cash and so security measures should be considered in the design and layout of this area.

FOH Storage

As with the stage and backstage areas, storage for the lobby is always required but often insufficient or lacking altogether. Among the items needed for the lobby and other FOH areas are: programs, posters, tables, chairs, stanchions, ticket stands, office supplies, janitorial supplies, banners, flags, food, beverage and concessions. It is best to include these spaces during design when they can be appropriately located. Remember, whether the storage is provided or not, these things will have to be put somewhere.

12 ADMINISTRATION

"Magic of the Theater" aside, theater is a business too and requires an administrative staff to program, manage, operate and maintain the facility. They are part of the team who, along with the performers, designers, stagehands, make a theater successful. Whenever possible, administrative offices should be within the facility with access to stage, backstage and front-of-house. Again, the size of the facility and the number of performance spaces will determine how many of what kind of administrative space will be needed, but some common spaces are noted below.

- Reception
- Copier, fax & mail
- Artistic director's office
- Business & development office
- Public relations office
- Food service manager's office
- Conference room
- Storage
- Staff lounge
- Staff restrooms

PROFIT AND LOSS STATEMENT FOR PERFORMING ARTS CENTER

REVENUE		Current Month	Year to Date
Project revenue		$304,830	$2,434,640
Other income		29,820	250,560
	Total Revenue	$334,650	$2,685,200
OPERATING EXPENSES			
Salaries: Direct		$121,725	$981,800
Indirect		28,392	343,241
Payroll taxes		4,653	37,224
Vacations		6,489	51,912
Sick leave		7,058	56,384
Holidays		9,355	74,840
Group insurance		1,100	8,880
General insurance		3,541	14,146
Printing & reproduction		8,400	66,780
Repairs & Maintenance		9,055	36,220
Supplies		6,703	26,812
Postage		9,468	

13 OUTSIDE THE BUILDING

It's obvious, but the first thing the audience sees is the outside of the theater. The design of the *façade* should be attractive and inviting. It can be a significant element in attracting audiences to the theater for performances and non-performance times. Certain features should be included for day-to-day operations and to attract theater-goers.

Marquee/Signs

Historically the theater marquee is located above the main entrance and identifies the name of the theater and the name of the attraction currently performing. It also creates the identity of the theater. This is appropriate when a theater is built in an urban area and fronts directly on to the street (as with most Broadway theaters).

Figure 53: Shubert Theater marquee.

If the theater is not visible from the main access road, then another marquee should be located where it can be seen. These remote signs are often electronic and can be used for advertising. You can't attract an audience if they can't find the theater – or don't even know it is there! This problem often occurs in facilities located on college campuses where the theater may be located within another building. Directions to the theater should be included on all campus signage and maps.

Performing arts centers, containing several different venues, will identify the name of the facility outside and the performances taking place in individual venues will be identified elsewhere. Signage should be located along all roadways that lead to the theater.

Poster Boxes

Poster boxes, identifying current and upcoming performances can be recessed into the face of the building or be free-standing. In either case, they should be illuminated and positioned to provide maximum visibility.

Figure 54: Metropolitan Opera poster boxes.

Landscaping/Seating

Landscaping and areas to sit are elements that make the theater an attractive destination. If the site permits, an outdoor plaza should be considered. A park-like environment will attract people during the day and evening. A plaza can accommodate concessions, food and beverages, outdoor performances and other events.

Drive-through

Also known as a *port cochère*, a drive-through allows persons to be dropped-off in front of the theater before a performance and for valet parking. Provision for short-term parking (15 minutes) is convenient for persons purchasing tickets during the day and for small front-of-house deliveries. The drive-through should direct vehicles from the theater directly to the parking area.

Parking

Theaters outside of urban areas must often consider parking in the initial planning and budgeting of the facility. Sometimes, an adjacent public parking facility can be used (as it will be mostly empty during the evening.) If shared parking is not available, then a parking structure will be required adjacent to or below the theater. In either case, ADA spaces must be provided. Convenient circulation (for persons-with-disabilities and able-bodied persons) from parking to the theater should be incorporated into the overall site plan of the facility. The architect usually addresses these issues but there are also parking and traffic consultants available for unique or difficult situations. In terms of quantity, a general rule-of-thumb is that there should be one parking space for every two seats in the theater.

Emergency Access

Access and dedicated parking for ambulance, fire trucks and other emergency vehicles should be provided at the entrance to the theater and adjacent to the loading dock.

14 PHYSICAL PLANT

Space for ducts, pipes, conduit, etc. are addressed by the architect and engineers during design and are not an issue except when they conflict with acoustic or theatrical concerns. This having been said, it is not a good idea to be too 'flip' about the mechanical systems. As you should be aware by this point, a theater is a very unique and complex building: all of whose systems must be integrated and coordinated for it to function properly. Everything in the building is intertwined and a seemingly small change or modification to one aspect can ripple through the entire building design as well as the building budget. The architect, mechanical engineer, theater consultant and most prominently, the acoustician will spend many, many hours reviewing duct routing, for example, to make sure noise and vibration criteria are met.

Customary design details and installation procedures for an office building or apartment block will not be suitable for a theater and the acoustician will provide proper details for all members of the design team to incorporate into their work. Having a properly detailed and coordinated set of drawings, however, is not a guarantee. Contractors and sub-contractors are often unfamiliar with the construction tolerances and procedures necessary in a theater. Oftimes, a worker faced with an unfamiliar product or procedure may be tempted to take a short-cut to save themselves time and effort, thinking that it won't matter and that nobody will know. It *will* matter and eventually everyone will know. The contractors and their staff and crew must fully understand both the letter and intent of the contract drawings to prevent mistakes. There should be regular inspections by members of the design team to answer questions and assure proper execution of the design.

Some of the other invisible spaces are noted below.
- Mechanical and electrical rooms
- Maintenance engineer's office
- Maintenance staff locker room
- Telephone gear room
- Fire control gear room
- IT gear room

- Transformer vault
- Stand-by generator and fuel tanks

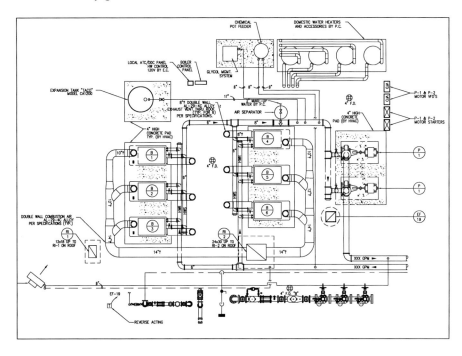

15 FINAL THOUGHTS

With this book, I have tried to create a useful guide for those 'crazy enough to try to build a theater'. It contains over 30 years of my life as a lighting designer, stage hand, theater consultant. I am what my father would have called a "theater buff". I find any and all aspects of theater fascinating and of interest. It is a lens for viewing the world. It describes a process that can last from two-to-six years or longer; not including the time required beforehand to make the initial decision, raise political capital, raise construction capital, find a site, etc. It is also an adventure through familiar and unfamiliar terrain that will require the coordinated efforts of hundreds (and sometimes thousands) of people. It will require a consensus among these people, each with their unique ideas and contributions, about what this particular theater will be/should be.

While the book contains lots of information it is not a 'manual' for creating a theater, nor should it be used as one. It is also not the only path to the creation of a theater; as I am constantly reminded when someone points out a design solution that is more elegant than mine! As with most things in this world, there are always different ways to proceed. What is most important, I believe, is to be patient and keep an open mind to all possibilities so that the process is enjoyable. Not that there won't be any bumps in the road: all long term collaborative endeavors inevitably have those moments when you wish you could be anywhere else in the world except in this room; with these people. Grrrr. There will also be epiphanies, moments of camaraderie and friendships that may continue long after completion of the project. In short, its life; it's a human endeavor that's been around as long as people have. It's challenging, creative, invigorating and fun; and if you're not having fun, why bother at all?

GLOSSARY

Acting area	The area of the stage used by performers.
ADA	The Americans with Disabilities Act (designed to ensure access to persons with disabilities).
ADAAG	The Americans with Disabilities Act Accessibility Guidelines (provides specific standards and details for implementation of the ADA).
AIA	American Institute of Architects.
Apron	The area directly in front of the proscenium opening (nearest the audience; a.k.a. forestage).
Arena	A stage with seating on four sides.
ASA	Acoustical Society of America.
As-Built	Plans created at the end of construction to represent the way the building was actually built (including all modifications and change orders).
ASME	American Society of Mechanical Engineers.
ASTC	American Society of Theater Consultants.
ASTM	American Society for Testing of Materials.
AWG	American Wire Guide.
Backstage	The areas adjacent to the stage but not visible to the audience (dressing rooms, loading dock, etc.).
Batten	A steel pipe that is part of the counterweight rigging system, that scenery, lighting, etc. is attached to (a.k.a. pipe batten or pipe).
BOCA	The Building Officials & Code Administrators National Building Code.
Boom	Any vertical pipe used for stage lighting.
Box boom	Vertical pipe used for stage lighting that is, historically, located in a seating box on the side of the auditorium. A generic term, today, for any side lighting position.
Call board	A bulletin board located at the stage door or near the green room. Cast and crew "calls" (schedules) are posted as well as other notices.

Catwalk	A technical access-way that may or may not support stage lighting fixtures; it is usually found above the audience seating area (for front lighting) or adjacent to the stage.
C.O.	Certificate of Occupancy (Issued by the building inspector with jurisdiction to certify that the completed facility meets all codes. The building can not legally be occupied without a C.O.).
Code	The municipal, state or federal guidelines for the design and construction of all buildings (a.k.a. building code).

Continental seating
A seating arrangement not interrupted by aisles.

Counterweight rigging
A system of rigging whereby the load of lights, scenery, etc. is counterbalanced see Single Purchase System and Double Purchase System.

Counterweight arbor
The arbor (or carriage) that holds the counterweights, that in turn counterbalance the load on the batten.

Cross Aisle	A large aisle running parallel to the stage used as an entryway into the theater (commonly used as a path of egress between a sloped seating area and a stepped seating area).
Cross-over	A hallway, outside of the stagehouse, to allow performers to move from one side of the stage to the other without being seen.
CSI	Construction Specifications Institute.
Cyclorama	("Cyc" and pronounced *sike*) an off-white or blue muslin cloth hung at the rear of the set or surrounding the set. The use of lighting and scenic projections can create the illusion of infinite distance or any other image desired.

Dead-hung	A light or piece of scenery that is suspended from a fixed location, and that cannot be raised or lowered.
Dead load	The net weight of a piece of structure (i.e. how much it weighs without anyone or anything on it).
Depression	The distance a concrete sub-floor is dropped to accommodate the finished floor assembly.
Diversity	(Electrical) a factor applied when designing the power requirements of the dimming system. Since it is very unlikely that all dimmers

will be simultaneously fully loaded and at full intensity; the power requirement can be reduced.

Diversity   (Structural) a factor applied when designing the infrastructure for the rigging system. Since it is very unlikely that all rigging battens will fully loaded, for a given production, the required weight and shape of the steel can be modified.

Double Purchase System
A counterweight rigging system that is counterbalanced on a 2:1 ratio. Each 100 pounds of load is balanced by 200 pounds of counterweight and for every foot the batten travels, the arbor travels ½ foot. The advantage to this system is that the counterweight travel is reduced by half, allowing the loading rail to be located on a gallery above the stage floor. The disadvantage is a slightly reduced efficiency in the set and the requirement of more counterweights, longer arbors and more time to load and unload a rigging set.

Downstage   Toward the front of the stage (toward the audience).

Drop   (Scenic drop) any full-stage, painted scene cloth typically used to provide a backdrop for the action on stage. Drops are suspended from the stage rigging.

Egress   A path leading to an exit.

Elevation   The height above or below an arbitrary point established for the building (usually the stage).

FC   The abbreviation for foot candles, which is a measurement of illumination.

Fire curtain   An intumescent curtain located immediately behind (upstage) the proscenium arch designed to intercept smoke, flames and hot gases.

Floor drop   A painted canvas or muslin drop laid on the stage floor as part of the design.

Fly gallery   A platform above the stage on the side containing the counterweight rigging system.

Fly loft/Stage-house
The area directly above the stage, housing the grid, rigging steel, counterweight rigging, etc.

FOH	(Front Of House) A generic term for areas of the theater other than the stage and backstage spaces; usually referring to the audience seating area or the lobby.
Gallery	Any platform on either side of, and above, the stage.
Glazing	Another word for glass.
Grade	The level of the soil surrounding the theater building (above grade is above ground and below grade is below ground).
Green room	A lounge for performers.
Gridiron/Grid	A steel working platform above the stage used for rigging.
Hand line	The operating line for the counterweight rigging system.
Head Block	A multi-groove sheave that gathers all the lift lines and routes them to the counterweight arbor.
Hemp rigging	A system of rigging whereby scenery, lighting, etc. is suspended; with minimal counterbalancing (usually sandbags).
House curtain	The main curtain, located directly upstage of the fire curtain, that may be raised or lowered to reveal or conceal the stage.
HVAC	**H**eating, **V**entilation and **A**ir **C**onditioning.
IALD	International Association of Lighting Designers.
IBC	The International Building Code (created as a national standard in lieu of regional codes such as BOCA and UBC).
IES	Illuminating Engineering Society.
Index strip light	
	A lighting fixtures suspended over the locking rail (to provide illumination of the locking rail during performances).
Lift lines	Fabricated from aircraft cable, they connect the batten to the arbor.
Live load	The weight of persons and equipment expected upon a piece of structure. For example, a lighting catwalk may have a "dead load" of only 10#/SF but a live load of 75#/SF (to accommodate stagehands, lighting fixtures, cable, etc.).

Loading gallery

Located below the headblock steel, it provides storage for counterweights and a location to load them onto the arbor.

Locking rail   A railing; running the length of the T-bar battery, that supports the rope locks.

Loft Block   A single groove sheave that directs the lift line from the headblock down to the batten.

Masking   Velour draperies placed above and to the side of the acting area (to mask the wings).

MasterSpec   Prepared by the CSI, this is the numbering system used to identify and coordinate the specifications used to describe the construction of the building.

Mechanical systems

Include plumbing, sprinklers and HVAC.

NEMA   National Electrical Manufacturers Association.

NEC   The National Electrical Code (USA).

NFPA 101   The National Life Safety Code, an adjunct to the IBC).

NIMBY   Not In My Back Yard.

Orchestra lift   A motorized lift located downstage (toward the audience) of the proscenium that can be placed at stage level, audience level or below audience level (to create an orchestra pit).

Orchestra pit   An area downstage of the proscenium below the audience level and, usually, partially under the stage for an orchestra.

Orchestra shell   A portable enclosure consisting of wall panels and ceiling panels that surrounds an orchestra performing in a proscenium theater.

OSHA   Occupational Safety and Hazard Association.

Pin rail   A steel structure used to tie-off spot lines and dead-hung rigging.

Pipe grid   A dead-hung assembly that supports stage lighting in studio and black box theaters. Typically fabricated from 1.5" steel pipe and arranged to create 4-6 foot modules, above the room.

Plaster line   A reference line running across the proscenium opening along the upstage wall (of the proscenium).

Port cochère	A drive through .
PSF	Pound per Square Foot.
PSI	Pound per Square Inch.
Proscenium	The picture frame opening between the stage and audience (through which the action is revealed).
Road house	A theater designed to accommodate touring attractions that will bring theatrical equipment with them.
RCP	Reflected Ceiling Plan used to locate all lighting fixtures.
Refuge area	An area designed for safety in case of fire (for persons who may not be able to exit the building).
RFI	Request of Information (issued by a contractor seeking clarification of an item).
Rigging steel	Structural steel designed to accept the headblocks, loftblocks, etc. and their associated loading.
Rise	The increase or decrease in slope of a horizontal surface (such as an aisle).
Riser	The vertical distance from one step to the next (usually between 4-7").
Rope lock	A lever that locks the hand line in place and prevents the batten from moving.
Scale	A drawing convention where a fraction of an inch, on a drawing, will represent one foot. (¼" scale would indicate that every ¼" on the drawing is equivalent to 1'-0").
Set-Back	A code requirement that a building not be sited directly on the property line. It must be set back some prescribed distance.
Sheave	A component of the counterweight rigging system used to guide the batten lift lines from the arbor to the batten.
Sightline	The ability of each audience member to see the stage without obstruction from persons seated in front (in both horizontal and vertical planes).
Single Purchase System	
	A counterweight rigging system that is counterbalanced on a 1:1 ratio. Each 100 pounds of load is balanced by 100 pounds of counterweight and for every foot the batten travels, the arbor travels one foot.

Site plan	A plan of the entire site including all buildings, roads, adjacent buildings and other significant elements.
Smoke pocket	A steel channel on either side of the proscenium that forms a smoke seal when the fire curtain is lowered.
Spot-line set	A dedicated rigging set, not part of the counterweight rigging, used to suspend a single item or a batten that is not parallel to the plaster line. These sets are typically rigged from the fly floor.
Stage right	The area to the performer's right (and the audience's left).
Staggered seating	
	An arrangement whereby the seats in alternate rows are offset to permit sightlines.
Stage left	The area to the performer's left (and the audience's right).
Standard seating	
	A seating arrangement with aisles every 14 seats.
STC	Sound Transmission Coefficient.
T-bar guide battery	
	A system of guides for the counterweight arbors.
Thrust stage	A stage with seating on three sides.
Tread	The horizontal surface of a stair (usually 11").
Trim	The desired position of a batten or piece of scenery (a.k.a. play position).
UBC	The Uniform Building Code (USA).
Upstage	Toward the rear of the stage (away from the audience).
Valance	A stage drapery used to adjust the height of the proscenium opening.
Wing	The stage areas directly offstage of the proscenium opening.

PICTURE CREDITS

FIGURE	CAPTION	CREDIT
Figure 1	Amphitheatre	Toga Sanbo, Japan
Figure 2	Detail of space plan	Theater Design
Figure 3	Typical Project Budget	Public Assembly Facilities, 3rd ed. 2003
Figure 4	Architect check-list	Public Assembly Facilities, 3rd ed. 2003
Figure 5	Sample RFQ	Theater Design
Figure 6	Sample RFP	Theater Design
Figure 7	55th Street Dance Theater	Robert Lorelli Associates
Figure 8	Benedum Center	Pittsburgh Trust for Cultural Resources
Figure 9	Nadine McGuire Theatre & Dance Pavilion	Zeidler Partnership Architects
Figure 10	Sala São Paolo	Theater Design
	Greek Theater at Epidaurus	Theatres & Opera Houses
	Reconstruction of Roman Theater at Ostia	Fragments d'Arachitecture Antique 1901
	Valenciennes Passion Play 1547	Bibliothèque Nationale, Paris
	Scena Tragica 1545	Sebastian Serlio
	Elizabethan Theater	Teatro, 1991
	Spanish Theater	Teatro, 1991
	Theatre Royal	Keith Mindham
	Wagner's Theater at Bayreuth	Theatres & Opera Houses
	Scene by Adolphe Appia	Foundation Adolphe Appia, Berne
	Scene by Edward Gordon Craig	Stage Yearbook, 1914
	Plan of Grosses Schaupielhaus	Architectura Teatra, 1947
	Gropius' Total Theater	Architectura Teatra, 1947
Figure 11	Bubble diagram	Theater Design
Figure 12	Cut-outs	Zeidler Partnership Architects
Figure 13	Cicely Tyson Fine & Performing Arts School	NJ K-12 Architects
Figure 14	Reflected Ceiling Plan	Theater Design

Figure 15	CSI Division Titles	Construction Specification Institute
Figure 16	Architect's stamp	Silverman Cosentino Associates
Figure 17	Addendum	Theater Design
Figure 18	Value engineering opportunities	Donnell Consultants Inc.
Figure 19	Kabuki Theater	Teatro, 1972
Figure 20	Nadine McGuire Pavilion during construction	Theater Design
Figure 21	RFI	Theater Design
Figure 22	Change Order	Theater Design
Figure 23	Site visit	Theater Design
Figure 24	Punch list	Theater Design
Figure 25	Generic Lighting system	Theater Design
Figure 26	Counterweight rigging system	J.R. Clancy
Figure 27	Floor mounted seating	Irwin Seating
Figure 28	Sound system block diagram	Theater Design
Figure 29	Sound system conduit layout	Theater Design
Figure 30	Orchestra lift	GALA
Figure 31	Theater forms	Theater Design
Figure 32	Stage floor details	Theater Design
Figure 33	Generic stage diagram	Theater Design
Figure 34	Circulation diagram	Theater Design
Figure 35	Chorus Dressing room	Theater Design
Figure 36	Nadine McGuire dance studio	Zeidler Partnership Architects
Figure 37	Generic scene shop	Theater Design
Figure 38	Generic costume shop	Theater Design
Figure 39	Dimmer rack	ETC
Figure 40	Orchestra pit	Theatres & Opera Houses, 1999
Figure 41	Loading dock diagram	Architectural Graphic Standards, 5th ed. 1956
Figure 42	Hammerstein Theatre	Artec Consultants

Figure 43a	No sightlines	Theater Design
Figure 43b	Every-other-row sightlines	Theater Design
Figure 43c	Every-row sightlines	Theater Design
Figure 44	Egress Plan	NJ K-12 Architects
Figure 45	Wheelchair space requirements	International Building Code, 2003
Figure 46	Assisted Listening system requirement	International Building Code, 2003
Figure 47	Sound & light lock	Theater Design
Figure 48	Center-line section	Theater Design
Figure 49	Lighting catwalk	Theater Design
Figure 50	Metropolitan Opera Lobby	Theater Design
Figure 51	Coat room	Theater Design
Figure 52	NY State Theater Box Office	Theater Design
Figure 53	Shubert Theater marquee	Theater Design
Figure 54	Metropolitan Opera poster boxes	Theater Design

BIBLIOGRAPHY

The following books, articles and periodicals will provide the interested reader with additional information. Please note that the titles listed below represent only a limited bibliography of books written in English. Many, many more titles are available and in other languages as well.

Books

*ABTT/DSA. **Technical Standards for Places of Entertainment**.* Entertainment Technology Press.

*Breton, Gaelle. **Theaters 1989 Editions du Moniteur**,* Paris. English edition by Princeton Architectural Press

*Broadway Live. **Stage Specs: A Technical Guide To Theatres**.* 1999 Edition. The League of American Theatres and Producers

*Brocket, Oscar G. **History of the Theatre**.*1968. Allyn and Bacon

*Brown, Catherine et al. **Building for the Arts**,* 1984, 1989. Western States Arts Federation

*Elder, Eldon. **Will It Make a Theatre**.* 1992. Americans For the Arts

*Evan Terry Associates, P.C. **Pocket Guide to the ADA, Americans with Disabilities Guidelines for Buildings and Facilities**,* 1997. John Wiley & Sons, Inc

*Golden, Joseph. **Help! A Guide to Seeking, Selecting and Surviving an Arts Consultant**.* 1963. NY Cultural Resources Council

*Golden, Joseph. **Olympus on Main Street: A Process for Planning a Community Arts Facility**.* 1980 Syracuse University Press

*Graham, Peter J. **Public Assembly Facility Management: Principles and Practices**,* 2004. International Association of Assembly Managers

*Hardin, Terri. **Theatres & Opera Houses**.* 1999. TODTRI Book Publishers

*Ham, Roderick. **Theatres**.* 1988. Elsevier Science & Technology Books

*Ham, Roderick. **Theatre Planning**.* 1972. University of Toronto Press

*Hardy, Hugh. **Building Type Basics for performing arts facilities**.* 2006 John Wiley & Sons, Inc.

*Izenour, George C. **Theater Design 2nd Edition**.* 1996. Yale University Press

*Izenour, George C. **Theater Technology 2nd Edition**.* 1996. Yale University Press

Jewel, Don. **Public Assembly Facilities, 3rd Edition**. *2003.* International Association of Assembly Managers.

Madden, Turner. **Public Assembly Facility Law**. 1998. International Association of Assembly Managers.

Mell, Michael. **How to Generate Additional Revenue**. January 2000. Facility Manager

Kid Friendly Facilities Pave the Way for Audience of the Future. August/September 2004. Facility Manager

Molinari, Cesare. **Theatre Through The Ages**. 1972 McGraw-Hill Book Company

Ogawa, Toshiro. **Theatre Engineering and Stage Machinery**. Entertainment Technology Press

Petersen, David C. **Developing Sports, Convention and Performing Arts Centers, 3rd Edition**. 2001. Urban Land Institute

Pine, Joseph B. **The Experience Econony**, 1999. Harvard Business School Press

Reid, Francis. **ABC of Theatre Jargon**. Entertainment Technology Press

Shuppan, Miesei. **Theaters and Halls**. 1996. Puroto Gyarakushi

Webb, Duncan. **Running Theaters: Best Practices for Leaders & Managers**. 2005 Allworth Press

Periodicals

Architecture www.architecturemag.com

Architectural Record www.architecturalrecord.com

Auditoria www.auditoria.tv

Entertainment Technology www.etnow.com

Facility Manager www.iaam.org

Lighting and Sound America www.lightingandsoundamerica.com

Lighting Dimensions www.lightingdimensions.com

Live Design www.livedesignmag.com

PLSN www.plsn.com

Rental & Staging www.uemedia.com

Sightline (UK) www.abtt.org.uk

Sightlines www.usitt.org

Sound & Communications www.testa.com

Stage Directions www.stage-directions.com

Theatre Design & Technology www.usitt.org

Venues Today www.venuestoday.com

ORGANIZATIONS

The following organizations are useful sources of information on various aspects of designing and operating theaters and the persons who work in them.

Association of British Theatre Technicians (ABTT) www.abtt.org.uk

American Institute of Architects (AIA) www.aia.org

American Society of Theatre Consultants (ASTC) www.theatreconsultants.org

American Symphony Orchestra League (ASOL) www.symphony.org

Americans for the Arts www.artsusa.org

Association of Performing Arts Presenters www.artspresenters.org

Association for Theatre in Higher Education (ATHE) www.athe.org

Audio Engineering Society (AES) www.aes.org

Australian Performing Arts Centre Association www.apac.com.au

Canadian Arts Presenting Association www.capacoa.ca

Canadian Institute for Theatre Technology (CITT) www.citt.org

Entertainment Services & Technology Association (ESTA) www.esta.org

Illuminating Engineering Society (IES) www.ies.org

International Association of Assembly Managers (IAAM) www.iaam.org

International Alliance of Theatrical Stage Employees (IATSE) www.iatse-intl.org

International Theatre Institute www.iti-worldwide.org

International Organization of Scenographers, Theater Architects and Technicians (OISTAT) www.oistat.org

International Society of Performing Arts (ISPA) www.ispa.org

League of Historic American Theatres (LHAT) www.lhat.org

Professional Association of Canadian Theatres www.pact.ca

Society of Theatre Consultants (UK) www.theatreconsultants.org.uk

Theatre Communications Group (TCG) www.tcg.org

United States Institute of Theatre Technology (USITT) www.usitt.org

United Scenic Artists (USA) www.usa829.org

VENDORS

The following list includes fims in the US and England, and is not anywhere close to exhaustive – nor is it meant to be. Comprehensive lists can be found in the annual directories published by *Lighting Dimensions*, *Live Design*, *Pro Light & Staging News* and *Sound & Communications* and on the Internet. A few of the major players are noted below.

Lighting

Altman Lighting www.altmanlighting.com
Arri (GB) Ltd www.arri.com
Avolites www.avolites.com
Barbizon www.barbizon.com
CCT Lighting www.cctlighting.com
DeSisti www.desisti.it
Electronic Theatre Controls (ETC) www.etcconnect.com
Lycian www.lycian.com
Lighting and Electronics www.l&e.com
NSI/Colortran www.colortan.com
PRG www.prg.com
Robert Juliat www.robertjuliat.fr
Strand Lighting www.strandlight.com
Strong www.strongint.com
White Light www.whitelight.ltd.uk

Rigging

GALA www.galainfo.com
Hall Stage www.hallstage.com
I Weiss www.iweiss.com
JOEL www.joelrigging.com
JR Clancy www.jrclancy.com
Peter Albrecht Company www.peteralbrecht.com

Pook, Diemont, Ohl www.pdoinc.com
Protech www.protech.com
Secoa www.secoa.com
Serapid www.serapid.com
Syracuse Scenery and Stage Lighting www.ssl.com
Texas Scenic www.texasscenic.com
Tiffen Scenic Studio www.tiffen.com

Sound
Marquee Audio Ltd www.marqueeaudio.co.uk

Peerson Audio www.peersonaudio.com
Engineering Harmonics www.engineeringharmonics.com
Rosner Custom Sound Rosner@aol.com
Sound by Design www.soundbydesign.net

Seating
American Seating www.americanseating.com
Ducharme Seating www.ducharmeseating.com
Hussey Seating www.husseyseating.com
Irwin Seating www.irwinseating.com
JG Seating www.jgseating.com
Theater Solutions www.theatersolutions.net

Miscellaneous
SICO www.sico.com
Stage Technologies www.stagetech.com
Stageright www.stageright.com
Virco www.virco.com
Wenger www.wengercorp.com

INDEX

ENTERTAINMENT TECHNOLOGY PRESS

FREE SUBSCRIPTION SERVICE

Keeping Up To Date with

Building Better Theaters

Entertainment Technology titles are continually up-dated, and all major changes and additions are listed in date order in the relevant dedicated area of the publisher's website. Simply go to the front page of www.etnow.com and click on the BOOKS button. From there you can locate the title and be connected through to the latest information and services related to the publication.

The author of the title welcomes comments and suggestions about the book and can be contacted by email at: mmell@theaterdesigninc.com

Titles Published by Entertainment Technology Press

ABC of Theatre Jargon *Francis Reid* **£9.95** ISBN 1904031099
This glossary of theatrical terminology explains the common words and phrases that are used in normal conversation between actors, directors, designers, technicians and managers.

Aluminium Structures in the Entertainment Industry *Peter Hind* **£24.95**
ISBN 1904031064
Aluminium Structures in the Entertainment Industry aims to educate the reader in all aspects of the design and safe usage of temporary and permanent aluminium structures specific to the entertainment industry – such as roof structures, PA towers, temporary staging, etc.

AutoCAD – A Handbook for Theatre Users *David Ripley* **£24.95** ISBN 1904031315
From 'Setting Up' to 'Drawing in Three Dimensions' via 'Drawings Within Drawings', this compact and fully illustrated guide to AutoCAD covers everything from the basics to full colour rendering and remote plotting.

Basics – A Beginner's Guide to Lighting Design *Peter Coleman* **£9.95** ISBN 1904031412
The fourth in the author's 'Basics' series, this title covers the subject area in four main sections: The Concept, Practical Matters, Related Issues and The Design Into Practice. In an area that is difficult to be definitive, there are several things that cross all the boundaries of all lighting design and it's these areas that the author seeks to help with.

Basics – A Beginner's Guide to Special Effects *Peter Coleman* **£9.95** ISBN 1904031331
This title introduces newcomers to the world of special effects. It describes all types of special effects including pyrotechnic, smoke and lighting effects, projections, noise machines, etc. It places emphasis on the safe storage, handling and use of pyrotechnics.

Basics – A Beginner's Guide to Stage Lighting *Peter Coleman* **£9.95** ISBN 190403120X
This title does what it says: it introduces newcomers to the world of stage lighting. It will not teach the reader the art of lighting design, but will teach beginners much about the 'nuts and bolts' of stage lighting.

Basics: A Beginner's Guide to Stage Management *Peter Coleman* **£7.95**
ISBN 9781904031475
The fifth in Peter Coleman's popular 'Basics' series, this title provides a practical insight into, and the definition of, the role of stage management. Further chapters describe Cueing or 'Calling' the Show (the Prompt Book), and the Hardware and Training for Stage Management. This is a book about people and systems, without which most of the technical equipment used by others in the performance workplace couldn't function.

Basics – A Beginner's Guide to Stage Sound *Peter Coleman* **£9.95** ISBN 1904031277
This title does what it says: it introduces newcomers to the world of stage sound. It will not teach the reader the art of sound design, but will teach beginners much about the background to sound reproduction in a theatrical environment.

Building Better Theaters *Michael Mell* **£16.95** 1904031404
A title within our Consultancy Series, this book describes the process of designing a theater,

from the initial decision to build through to opening night. Michael Mell's book provides a step-by-step guide to the design and construction of performing arts facilities. Chapters discuss: assembling your team, selecting an architect, different construction methods, the architectural design process, construction of the theater, theatrical systems and equipment, the stage, backstage, the auditorium, ADA requirements and the lobby. Each chapter clearly describes what to expect and how to avoid surprises. It is a must-read for architects, planners, performing arts groups, educators and anyone who may be considering building or renovating a theater.

Case Studies in Crowd Management
Chris Kemp, Iain Hill, Mick Upton, Mark Hamilton **£16.95** ISBN 9781904031482
This important work has been compiled from a series of research projects carried out by the staff of the Centre for Crowd Management and Security Studies at Buckinghamshire Chilterns University College, and seminar work carried out in Berlin and Groningen with partner Yourope. It includes case studies, reports and a crowd management safety plan for a major outdoor rock concert, safe management of rock concerts utilising a triple barrier safety system and pan-European Health & Safety Issues.

Close Protection – The Softer Skills *Geoffrey Padgham* **£11.95** ISBN 1904031390
This is the first educational book in a new 'Security Series' for Entertainment Technology Press, and it coincides with the launch of the new 'Protective Security Management' Foundation Degree at Buckinghamshire Chilterns University College (BCUC). The author is a former full-career Metropolitan Police Inspector from New Scotland Yard with 27 years' experience of close protection (CP). For 22 of those years he specialised in operations and senior management duties with the Royalty Protection Department at Buckingham Palace, followed by five years in the private security industry specialising in CP training design and delivery. His wealth of protection experience comes across throughout the text, which incorporates sound advice and exceptional practical guidance, subtly separating fact from fiction. This publication is an excellent form of reference material for experienced operatives, students and trainees.

A Comparative Study of Crowd Behaviour at Two Major Music Events
Chris Kemp, Iain Hill, Mick Upton **£7.95** ISBN 1904031250
A compilation of the findings of reports made at two major live music concerts, and in particular crowd behaviour, which is followed from ingress to egress.

Copenhagen Opera House *Richard Brett and John Offord* **£32.00** ISBN 1904031420
Completed in a little over three years, the Copenhagen Opera House opened with a royal gala performance on 15th January 2005. Built on a spacious brown-field site, the building is a landmark venue and this book provides the complete technical background story to an opera house set to become a benchmark for future design and planning. Sixteen chapters by relevant experts involved with the project cover everything from the planning of the auditorium and studio stage, the stage engineering, stage lighting and control and architectural lighting through to acoustic design and sound technology plus technical summaries.

Electrical Safety for Live Events *Marco van Beek* **£16.95** ISBN 1904031285
This title covers electrical safety regulations and good pracitise pertinent to the entertainment industries and includes some basic electrical theory as well as clarifying the "do's and don't's" of working with electricity.

The Exeter Theatre Fire *David Anderson* **£24.95** ISBN 1904031137
This title is a fascinating insight into the events that led up to the disaster at the Theatre Royal, Exeter, on the night of September 5th 1887. The book details what went wrong, and the lessons that were learned from the event.

Fading Light – A Year in Retirement *Francis Reid* **£14.95** ISBN 1904031358
Francis Reid, the lighting industry's favourite author, describes a full year in retirement. "Old age is much more fun than I expected," he says. Fading Light describes visits and experiences to the author's favourite theatres and opera houses, places of relaxation and re-visits to scholarly intitutions.

Focus on Lighting Technology *Richard Cadena* **£17.95** ISBN 1904031145
This concise work unravels the mechanics behind modern performance lighting and appeals to designers and technicians alike. Packed with clear, easy-to-read diagrams, the book provides excellent explanations behind the technology of performance lighting.

The Followspot Guide *Nick Mobsby* **£28.95** ISBN 9781904031499
The first in ETP's Equipment Series, Nick Mobsby's Followspot Guide tells you everything you need to know about followspots, from their history through to maintenance and usage. It's pages include a technical specification of 193 followspots from historical to the latest 2007 versions from major manufacturers.

From Ancient Rome to Rock 'n' Roll – a Review of the UK Leisure Security Industry *Mick Upton* **£14.95** ISBN 9781904031505
From stewarding, close protection and crowd management through to his engagement as a senior consultant Mick Upton has been ever present in the events industry. A founder of ShowSec International in 1982 he was its chairman until 2000. The author has led the way on training within the sector. He set up the ShowSec Training Centre and has acted as a consultant at the Bramshill Police College. He has been prominent in the development of courses at Buckinghamshire New University where he was awarded a Doctorate in 2005. Mick has received numerous industry awards. His book is a personal account of the development and professionalism of the sector across the past 50 years.

Health and Safety Aspects in the Live Music Industry *Chris Kemp, Iain Hill* **£30.00**
ISBN 1904031226
This title includes chapters on various safety aspects of live event production and is written by specialists in their particular areas of expertise.

Health and Safety Management in the Live Music and Events Industry *Chris Hannam*
£25.95 ISBN 1904031307
This title covers the health and safety regulations and their application regarding all aspects of staging live entertainment events, and is an invaluable manual for production managers and event organisers.

Hearing the Light – 50 Years Backstage *Francis Reid* **£24.95** ISBN 1904031188
This highly enjoyable memoir delves deeply into the theatricality of the industry. The author's almost fanatical interest in opera, his formative period as lighting designer at Glyndebourne and his experiences as a theatre administrator, writer and teacher make for a broad and unique background.

An Introduction to Rigging in the Entertainment Industry *Chris Higgs* **£24.95**
ISBN 1904031129
This book is a practical guide to rigging techniques and practices and also thoroughly covers
safety issues and discusses the implications of working within recommended guidelines and
regulations.

Let There be Light – Entertainment Lighting Software Pioneers in Conversation
Robert Bell **£32.00** ISBN 1904031242
Robert Bell interviews a distinguished group of software engineers working on
entertainment lighting ideas and products.

Lighting for Roméo and Juliette *John Offord* **£26.95** ISBN 1904031161
John Offord describes the making of the Vienna State Opera production from the lighting
designer's viewpoint – from the point where director Jürgen Flimm made his decision not to
use scenery or sets and simply employ the expertise of LD Patrick Woodroffe.

Lighting Systems for TV Studios *Nick Mobsby* **£45.00** ISBN 1904031005
Lighting Systems for TV Studios, now in its second edition, is the first book specifically
written on the subject and has become the 'standard' resource work for studio planning
and design covering the key elements of system design, luminaires, dimming, control,
data networks and suspension systems as well as detailing the infrastructure items such as
cyclorama, electrical and ventilation. Sensibly TV lighting principles are explained and
some history on TV broadcasting, camera technology and the equipment is provided to
help set the scene! The second edition includes applications for sine wave and distributed
dimming, moving lights, Ethernet and new cool lamp technology.

Lighting Techniques for Theatre-in-the-Round *Jackie Staines* **£24.95**
ISBN 1904031013
Lighting Techniques for Theatre-in-the-Round is a unique reference source for those working
on lighting design for theatre-in-the-round for the first time. It is the first title to be published
specifically on the subject, it also provides some anecdotes and ideas for more challenging
shows, and attempts to blow away some of the myths surrounding lighting in this format.

Lighting the Stage *Francis Reid* **£14.95** ISBN 1904031080
Lighting the Stage discusses the human relationships involved in lighting design – both
between people, and between these people and technology. The book is written from a
highly personal viewpoint and its 'thinking aloud' approach is one that Francis Reid has
used in his writings over the past 30 years.

Model National Standard Conditions *ABTT/DSA/LGLA* **£20.00** ISBN 1904031110
These *Model National Standard Conditions* covers operational matters and complement *The
Technical Standards for Places of Entertainment*, which describes the physical requirements
for building and maintaining entertainment premises.

Mr Phipps' Theatre *Mark Jones, John Pick* **£17.95** ISBN: 1904031382
Mark Jones and John Pick describe "The Sensational Story of Eastbourne's Royal
Hippodrome" – formerly Eastbourne Theatre Royal. An intriguing narrative, the book sets
the story against a unique social history of the town. Peter Longman, former director of The
Theatres Trust, provides the Foreword.

Pages From Stages *Anthony Field* **£17.95** ISBN 1904031269
Anthony Field explores the changing style of theatres including interior design, exterior design, ticket and seat prices, and levels of service, while questioning whether the theatre still exists as a place of entertainment for regular theatre-goers.

Performing Arts Technical Training Handbook 2007/2008 *ed: John Offord* **£19.95** ISBN 9781904031451
Published in association with the ABTT (Association of British Theatre Technicians), this important Handbook includes fully detailed and indexed entries describing courses on backstage crafts offered by over 100 universities and colleges across the UK. A completely new research project, with accompanying website, the title also includes articles with advice for those considering a career 'behind the scenes', together with contact information and descriptions of the major organisations involved with industry training – plus details of companies offering training within their own premises. The Handbook will be kept in print, with a major revision annually.

Practical Dimming *Nick Mobsby* **£22.95** ISBN 19040313447
This important and easy to read title covers the history of electrical and electronic dimming, how dimmers work, current dimmer types from around the world, planning of a dimming system, looking at new sine wave dimming technology and distributed dimming. Integration of dimming into different performance venues as well as the necessary supporting electrical systems are fully detailed. Significant levels of information are provided on the many different forms and costs of potential solutions as well as how to plan specific solutions. Architectural dimming for the likes of hotels, museums and shopping centres is included. Practical Dimming is a companion book to Practical DMX and is designed for all involved in the use, operation and design of dimming systems.

Practical DMX *Nick Mobsby* **£16.95** ISBN 1904031368
In this highly topical and important title the author details the principles of DMX, how to plan a network, how to choose equipment and cables, with data on products from around the world, and how to install DMX networks for shows and on a permanently installed basis. The easy style of the book and the helpful fault finding tips, together with a review of different DMX testing devices provide an ideal companion for all lighting technicians and system designers. An introduction to Ethernet and Canbus networks are provided as well tips on analogue networks and protocol conversion. This title has been recently updated to include a new chapter on Remote Device Management that became an international standard in Summer 2006.

Practical Guide to Health and Safety in the Entertainment Industry
Marco van Beek **£14.95** ISBN 1904031048
This book is designed to provide a practical approach to Health and Safety within the Live Entertainment and Event industry. It gives industry-pertinent examples, and seeks to break down the myths surrounding Health and Safety.

Production Management *Joe Aveline* **£17.95** ISBN 1904031102
Joe Aveline's book is an in-depth guide to the role of the Production Manager, and includes real-life practical examples and 'Aveline's Fables' – anecdotes of his experiences with real messages behind them.

Rigging for Entertainment: Regulations and Practice *Chris Higgs* **£19.95**
ISBN 1904031218
Continuing where he left off with his highly successful *An Introduction to Rigging in the Entertainment Industry*, Chris Higgs' second title covers the regulations and use of equipment in greater detail.

Rock Solid Ethernet *Wayne Howell* **£24.95** ISBN 1904031293
Although aimed specifically at specifiers, installers and users of entertainment industry systems, this book will give the reader a thorough grounding in all aspects of computer networks, whatever industry they may work in. The inclusion of historical and technical 'sidebars' make for an enjoyable as well as informative read.

Sixty Years of Light Work *Fred Bentham* **£26.95** ISBN 1904031072
This title is an autobiography of one of the great names behind the development of modern stage lighting equipment and techniques.

Sound for the Stage *Patrick Finelli* **£24.95** ISBN 1904031153
Patrick Finelli's thorough manual covering all aspects of live and recorded sound for performance is a complete training course for anyone interested in working in the field of stage sound, and is a must for any student of sound.

Stage Lighting Design in Britain: The Emergence of the Lighting Designer, 1881-1950 *Nigel Morgan* **£17.95** ISBN 190403134X
This book sets out to ascertain the main course of events and the controlling factors that determined the emergence of the theatre lighting designer in Britain, starting with the introduction of incandescent electric light to the stage, and ending at the time of the first public lighting design credits around 1950. The book explores the practitioners, equipment, installations and techniques of lighting design.

Stage Lighting for Theatre Designers *Nigel Morgan* **£17.95** ISBN 1904031196
This is an updated second edition of Nigel Morgan's popular book for students of theatre design – outlining all the techniques of stage lighting design.

Technical Marketing Techniques *David Brooks, Andy Collier, Steve Norman* **£24.95** ISBN 190403103X
Technical Marketing is a novel concept, recently defined and elaborated by the authors of this book, with business-to-business companies competing in fast developing technical product sectors.

Technical Standards for Places of Entertainment *ABTT/DSA* **£30.00** ISBN 1904031056
Technical Standards for Places of Entertainment details the necessary physical standards required for entertainment venues.

Theatre Engineering and Stage Machinery *Toshiro Ogawa* **£30.00** ISBN 9781904031024
Theatre Engineering and Stage Machinery is a unique reference work covering every aspect of theatrical machinery and stage technology in global terms, and across the complete historical spectrum. Revised February 2007.

Theatre Lighting in the Age of Gas *Terence Rees* **£24.95** ISBN 190403117X
Entertainment Technology Press has republished this valuable historic work previously

produced by the Society for Theatre Research in 1978. *Theatre Lighting in the Age of Gas* investigates the technological and artistic achievements of theatre lighting engineers from the 1700s to the late Victorian period.

Theatre Space: A Rediscovery Reported *Francis Reid* **£19.95** ISBN 1904031439
In the post-war world of the 1950s and 60s, the format of theatre space became a matter for a debate that aroused passions of an intensity unknown before or since. The proscenium arch was clearly identified as the enemy, accused of forming a barrier to disrupt the relations between the actor and audience. An uneasy fellow-traveller at the time, Francis Reid later recorded his impressions whilst enjoying performances or working in theatres old and new and this book is an important collection of his writings in various theatrical journals from 1969-2001 including his contribution to the Cambridge Guide to the Theatre in 1988. It reports some of the flavour of the period when theatre architecture was rediscovering its past in a search to establish its future.

Theatres of Achievement *John Higgins* **£29.95** ISBN: 1904031374
John Higgins affectionately describes the history of 40 distinguished UK theatres in a personal tribute, each uniquely illustrated by the author. Completing each profile is colour photography by Adrian Eggleston.

Theatric Tourist *Francis Reid* **£19.95** ISBN 9781904031468
Theatric Tourist is the delightful story of Francis Reid's visits across more than 50 years to theatres, theatre museums, performances and even movie theme parks. In his inimitable style, the author involves the reader within a personal experience of venues from the Legacy of Rome to theatres of the Renaissance and Eighteenth Century Baroque and the Gustavian Theatres of Stockholm. His performance experiences include Wagner in Beyreuth, the Pleasures of Tivoli and Wayang in Singapore. This is a 'must have' title for those who are as "incurably stagestruck" as the author.

Walt Disney Concert Hall – The Backstage Story *Patricia MacKay & Richard Pilbrow* **£28.95** ISBN 1904031234
Spanning the 16-year history of the design and construction of the Walt Disney Concert Hall, this book provides a fresh and detailed behind the scenes story of the design and technology from a variety of viewpoints. This is the first book to reveal the "process" of the design of a concert hall.

Yesterday's Lights – A Revolution Reported *Francis Reid* **£26.95** ISBN 1904031323
Set to help new generations to be aware of where the art and science of theatre lighting is coming from – and stimulate a nostalgia trip for those who lived through the period, Francis Reid's latest book has over 350 pages dedicated to the task, covering the 'revolution' from the fifties through to the present day. Although this is a highly personal account of the development of lighting design and technology and he admits that there are 'gaps', you'd be hard put to find anything of significance missing.

Go to www.etbooks.co.uk for full details of above titles and secure online ordering facilities.